PUBLIC EDUCATION,
DEMOCRACY,
AND THE
COMMON GOOD

edited by
DONOVAN R. WALLING

Phi Delta Kappa Educational Foundation
Bloomington, Indiana U.S.A.

Cover design by
Victoria Voelker

Cover photograph by
Vladimir Bektesh

Phi Delta Kappa Educational Foundation
408 North Union Street
Post Office Box 789
Bloomington, IN 47402-0789
U.S.A.

Printed in the United States of America
Library of Congress Control Number 2004096107
ISBN 0-87367-854-0

TABLE OF CONTENTS

INTRODUCTION

The development of this volume of essays began with a proposition: In the early days of the American republic, universal public education was proposed as the surest support of the common good and the only institution that could ensure and sustain the good health of American democracy. Is this proposition still true today? If so, how should we act on this proposition — as educators, as citizens?

A number of writers have attempted to answer these questions. These essayists give voice to a range of responses, from the politically conservative to the politically liberal, from the theoretical to the practical in education. We have made no attempt to slant this collection in one direction or another, nor was balance an issue. We simply let the writers' biases, viewpoints, and philosophies fall where they might.

Admittedly, our *approach* to the topic could be characterized as "liberal" in the sense that Stephen P. Turner uses the term in his recent book, *Liberal Democracy 3.0* (Sage, 2003), when he writes,

> One way of interpreting the history of liberalism is to see it as the continual expansion of the circle of civility, of democratic participation in "government by discussion," so that more and more people participated in the discussion. (p. 97)

At this time in our national history, such discussion seems especially pertinent. Public education has been beset, and its harshest critics would see it abolished in favor of privatization schemes, both secular and religious.

Education is fundamental in any society. The common good of a society in large measure turns on what constitutes education and who gets the opportunity to learn and in what measure. Phi

Delta Kappa International, in accordance with its constitution and bylaws, historically has been "concerned with and directed toward the improvement of education, especially of publicly supported, universally available education." The association has embraced this mission since its founding in 1906. But "the character of Phi Delta Kappa in carrying forward programs, activities, and initiatives in support of the association's purpose shall be nonpolitical or nonpartisan to the greatest extent possible." Thus our intent in this volume is to foster discussion, not to promote a particular viewpoint or ideology.

We have chosen to view discussion not as a hallmark of "liberalism" per se, but as an essential element of democratic society. How else but by voice and vote do a civil people determine the boundaries and freedoms of their society? By providing a forum for these essays, our hope is to expand the national (at times international) discussion of how a democratic society ensures through education its future *as* a democratic society. Of course, this is a sweeping proposition. A full range of responses would take a much larger volume than this one. These writers present their views, their pieces of the mosaic of this topic. The result is fragmentary but, we hope, nonetheless compelling.

OUR SCHOOLS AS AN APPRENTICESHIP IN DEMOCRACY

JOHN I. GOODLAD

Just seven generations ago, a group of men laid out a bill of particulars regarding how we should govern ourselves and relate to one another into an indefinite future. The attention of the world was drawn to a unique experiment that promised to place this future in the hands of the people — no queens or kings, no lords or ladies, no caste system of prestige, privilege, and power.

They were not just observers abroad who were skeptical. Some of those Founding Fathers to whom we give credit also had their doubts. James Madison, for example, has been quoted as saying that "the people is a beast." The question of whether the citizens of this democracy could govern themselves hung like a cloud over the delegates at the Constitutional Convention of 1787.

European savants in particular feared the viruses of human nature — that those elected to public office would come to exhibit

John I. Goodlad earned his Ph.D. at the University of Chicago and has been awarded honorary doctorates by 20 colleges and universities in the United States and Canada. He is a senior fellow in the Teachers for a New Era Program at the University of Washington and president of the independent Institute for Educational Renewal in Seattle. His most recent books, all published in 2004, are *Romance with Schools,* a 20th anniversary edition of *A Place Called School, Education for Everyone: Agenda for Education in a Democracy* (with Corinne Mantle-Bromley and Stephen J. Goodlad), and *The Teaching Career* (co-edited with Timothy J. McMannon).

the same traits of aggrandizement as the tyrants of monarchist and totalitarian regimes. Some saw more of the right to individual freedom and justice in the documents than of responsibility for preserving both, more of democracy taking care of the people than of the people taking care of it. The French visitor to our shores half a century later, writer and statesman Alexis de Tocqueville, declared the fledgling democracy to be "an arduous apprenticeship of liberty."

In his vision of the future, it is unlikely that Thomas Jefferson saw a massive enterprise of universal public schooling as the major provider of this apprenticeship. But he did view ignorance as democracy's enemy and education as the answer: The simultaneous existence of both ignorance and democracy "never was, nor never will be."

The cloud that hung over Convention Hall has had its successors ever since. In 1949, a group of faculty members at the University of Chicago, deeply concerned about the people's stewardship of the democracy committed to their care, drafted a public alert: "If the United States is to be democracy, its citizens must be free. If citizens are to be free, they must be their own judges. If they are to judge well, they must be wise. Citizens may be born free; they are not born wise."[1]

In 2003, David Brooks wrote a sentence destined to provoke controversy: "In the building of free societies, every day feels like a mess, but every year is a step forward."[2] There probably has not been an era since the United States of America was born that has been absent of fear that our democratic experiment was slipping backward. Indeed, fear itself has been a catalyst of doubt regarding the strength of the major pillars supporting our democracy. Wendell Berry's essay, written in the early aftermath of September 11, 2001, struck a chord. Within a month after publication of his "Thoughts in the Presence of Fear," reprints appeared in dozens of publications reaching millions of people worldwide. In it, he wrote: "And surely, in our country, under our constitution, it is a fundamental error to suppose that any crisis or emergency can justify any form of political oppression"[3] — another sentence destined to create controversy.

Citizens differ in their views, as our Constitution says they should be free to do. Nonetheless, we must continually renew our understanding of and commitment to the associational and political democracy that binds us together as a nation.

The "beast" to which Madison referred has come a long way. Jefferson was right. Education, much of it provided in a near-universal system of public schooling, has served the nation well. But ironically, the sense of promise fulfilled in the ubiquitous cradle of a robust democracy has lulled many of us with the myth that it takes care of itself. We need only celebrate it.

In this short essay, I seek to carry the reader through three themes of my own learning and the accompanying development of an ecology of belief regarding the onion-like layers of complexity inherent in understanding and practicing democracy. The first has to do with the nature of democracy and education and the linkages between the two. The second addresses the thorny issue of building into the conduct of schooling a common mission for the individual and collective good. The third briefly describes the creation of and experience with an educational agenda for schooling that appears to offer some promise of serving the public good. It is a work in progress, as is democracy itself.

Coming to Democracy

Most of us came into the American democracy without knowing it. Most of the rest came knowingly, attracted particularly by the concepts of liberty and justice for all. For some who came, the attraction was prosperity; liberty and justice were value added. Kenneth Sirotnik nicely sums up the democracy we now have:

> America is a collection of multiple communities defined by different interests, races, ethnicities, regions, economic stratifications, religions, and so forth. Celebrating these differences is part of what makes this nation great. But there is a community — a moral community — that transcends the special interests of individuals, families, groups, that stands for what this nation is all about: liberty and *justice* for all. . . .

> It is a "moral ecology" held together by a political democ-
> racy and the fundamental values embedded in the system.[4]

Those born into this system learned bits and pieces about it growing up, much of this in schools. Immigrants learned a chunk of it preparing for and experiencing the naturalization process. Coming from Canada, I had in becoming an adult experienced the associational fabric of a democracy but not the political one framed by the Constitution.

I shall never forget that ceremony of naturalization a half-century ago in Atlanta. Most of the more than a hundred who became, with me, citizens on that day came from societies quite differently governed than Canada and the United States of America. The tears of joy, expressions such as "thank God," and jubilance of young and old told me a lot about the contrast between lives left and lives presumed to be dawning. I have thought often since about something similar for citizens born here — perhaps marking both graduation from high school and educational immersion in an apprenticeship of democracy.

This immersion would be into more than governance. "The fundamental values embedded in the system" embrace much more. The political philosopher Johannes Althusius nicely introduced a comprehensive conception early in the 17th century: "Politics is the art of associating men [sic] for the purpose of establishing, cultivating, and conserving social life among them. Whence it is called 'symbiotics'"[5] For him, symbiotics and symbioses included all human associations. But even this is not the full scope of the word *democracy* in my ecology of belief. It encompasses association with one's habitat as well.

A Habitat for Democracy

Just as we are not born with the desired traits of establishing, cultivating, and conserving associational life among us, our democracy did not give birth to their desirability. The great religions of the world have long taught the value of such dispositions as forgiveness, compassion, gratitude, honesty, and love. Divine and rational thought has for centuries stipulated overlapping values that define democratic association: equality, civility, fairness, justice, civicness, freedom, courage, community, and more.[6]

Parents with whom I have had conversations in this country and countries around the world expect schools to play a major role in developing these values in their children. Teaching these is what serves the public good by deliberately putting the moral into education, a concept that is morally neutral until the good or the bad, the moral or the immoral, is embedded in it. These are some of the values — particularly liberty and justice for all — that Sirotnik was thinking of as embedded in the moral ecology that binds us together in democratic community. They must be carefully taught to prevent us from "hating all the people our relatives hate" (to cite a line from the musical *South Pacific*) and all those others who differ from us in color, religion, sexual orientation, cultural norms, and the rest.

Just as these values are widely shared and have a long history, much of the same can be said about education as a moral endeavor and about schooling as a medium for its advancement. The highly influential neo-Confucian scholar and philosopher Chu Hsi viewed the schooling of his time — 12th century China — as too much oriented toward passing the civil service examinations at the expense of moral self-transformation.[7] Sound familiar?

A Host of "Everyones"

The early landowners in the northeast region of what is now the United States of America brought with them a sense of education as the medium for ensuring preservation of the values they held. This did not, however, include democratic belief in the individual's right to gain knowledge. Nonetheless, the intent was to serve a common good — to ensure that the immigrant "commoners" would learn the laws of the land and the associational precepts thought necessary to community. These would be commonly taught to the young in schools of strict discipline, the model they thought necessary for shaping moral adulthood.

Herein lay great challenges to the later conduct of democracy, education, and public schooling. These stern precepts were derived from the prevailing religion — the only religion of the tax-paying householders. Consequently, their assessments to support schools were self-serving, in both a private and a community sense, whether they sent their own children there, had them tutored, or, later, sent them off to private academies. The concept of schooling for the public good was born, albeit a narrow but all-encompassing good at the time.

Rapid increases in immigrants and in their diversity, including in religion, made controversial this concept of a common school but did not diminish the public need for a literate citizenry and hence the need for universal public schooling to provide it. But whose values, what values, were to prevail in the classroom? Is it any wonder that the Founding Fathers were unable to disperse the cloud hanging over Convention Hall? Benjamin Barber has neatly phrased the challenge that is still with us and will continue to be: "Our schools are public not just in that they must educate everyone, but in that they must turn a host of 'everyones' into something like a single national One: the civic entity we call a 'public.'"[8]

This is not the place to examine the wisdom that led to the separation of church and state as a fundamental principle of the American democracy. The absence of federal responsibility for education and schooling in the Constitution nonetheless left public education as a state function; therefore homes and religious institutions came to be seen as the primary educators of the young but not necessarily joined in educational purpose. Families and religious institutions have their own private purposes and are free to align them as they wish. However, they are not free to thrust this alignment on the public purpose of schooling. Nor are parents who withdraw their children from the public school free to withdraw their financial support of it.

These circumstances have contributed significantly to our difficulty in meeting the challenge summarized by Barber: crafting a clear mission of schooling, addressed to turning "a host of 'everyones' into something like a single national One." The conduct of public schooling is pushed this way and that by a cacophony of voices directed to the teaching of private purpose and, increasingly in recent years, of school failure. Ironically, the voices least heard are those seeking to tell us that the most serious failure has been that of the nation not ensuring for our schools — both public and private — a common mission of educating the young in democratic character and the freedoms and responsibilities of democratic citizenship. The presidential candidates in the 1992, 1996, and 2000 election debates said little to nothing about this public purpose of schooling.

There are many possible explanations for the absence of clear articulation of and commitment to this mission, even though studies and polls over many years reveal widespread public expectations for the schools to teach the very traits of character and citizenship a democratic mission of schooling calls for.[9] The devil is in the implementation — the transfer from the general to the specific in school practices.

The American Dream

At the general level, a basic principle of democracy is individual freedom of belief. Democracy requires a core of common values — justice, fairness, civility, and all the rest. These constitute its moral grounding. But they become very risk-laden concepts when attached to being taught to the young in public schools. Whose values? What morals? The synapses of the brain fail to flood one's mental space with the realization that, without a common core of values and belief, there is no culture. Without a culture, what will guide development of a sense of self? What, then, are to be the values and beliefs by which the morality of a democratic society and its citizens are to be judged? What is the good that must characterize the educational ecology of the young? And who are to be their citizen-educators?

These are tough questions. A richness of literature — of both the rational and the divine idiom — has addressed these over many centuries. There probably has been as much produced in the United States alone during the last two hundred years as in the entire world over the preceding millennia. But the necessary agenda for the educational apprenticeship of all our citizens in the understandings and behaviors necessary to a robust, renewing democracy still elude us. Perhaps, then, the American Dream is just that — a dream. Why not leave it there? Is it not the Dream that binds us together as a single national One of everyone?

Or is the dream itself a nonsensical, unrealistic fabrication? If so, let's leave it to those who enjoy fabricating it and get on with our practical affairs: finding dependable child care, looking after our economic well-being, fixing health care, tightening national security even if this means giving up some of our privacy and liberties, and making sure that our public schools are preparing young people to be dependable members of the workforce. Most of this necessary educating can be done electronically anyway. But it needs to be done in schools to keep the kids off the streets and out of our homes and shopping malls. We certainly do not need to involve our schools in promoting and sustaining our democracy. If that is what Thomas Jefferson had in mind, he was wrong.

Agenda for Education in a Democracy

In 1990, two colleagues — Kenneth Sirotnik and Roger Soder — and I released a trilogy of books reporting five years of inquiry centered on the education of educators for our schools.[10] One reported the findings, conclusions, and recommendations we had drawn from a nationwide representative sample of educator-preparing settings in the United States. Another provided, in considerable historical depth, teacher education in four clusters of our sample: small liberal arts colleges, former normal schools, private universities, and major public universities. The third, titled *The Moral Dimensions of Teaching*, stirred the most lively response, both here and abroad.

Early on, queries regarding this third volume focused on the word *moral*. What morals? Whose morals? Clearly, the questioners had not read the book. Some equated the word with individual behavior regarding alcohol, drugs, and sex. Religious fundamentalists saw us as allies in spreading the word of God. Months later, questions from people who obviously had read the book addressed such issues as the relationship among democracy, education, and "the moral." Educators in Moscow, following the implosion of the USSR, were looking to the book for guides into the role of education in the structuring of a Russian democracy. Some philosophically inclined educators in the United States viewed our perspective as invigorating discourse about education as a moral endeavor, frequently citing the contributions of John Dewey.

Education philosopher Donna Kerr had helped us select a group of educators — mostly historians and philosophers — who represented competence in an array of themes focusing on the role of teachers and schools in developing what we later referred to as democratic character.[11] Our work together contributed significantly to Ken, Roger, and I crafting an agenda for schooling and the education of its primary stewards: Agenda for Education in a Democracy.

The Agenda grew out of much more than this five-year period of inquiry. Ken and I had engaged in two other multi-year comprehensive studies: one on school change involving a network of schools in southern California known as the League of Cooperating Schools, and the other, A Study of Schooling in the United States, on a purposively representative sample of schools nationwide. Two major findings significantly influenced the design of our Study of the Education of Educators, for which Roger joined us at the University of Washington. We found in none of the schools studied an ongoing process of renewal of the kind necessary to changing much more than daily routines.

Given this omission, a second finding, although disturbing, was not at all surprising: These schools were not engaged in any overarching mission of public educational purpose. The teachers, under the leadership of the principals, certainly were not asking themselves whether their daily teaching of mathematics, literature, social studies, science, and the rest was deliberately contributing to the personal and social development of the young, as the public has come to expect of our schools.

Were these representative educators not prepared in their own professional development programs for creating cultures of continuous renewal, guided by a public purpose of schooling in our democracy? This is one of the major questions we sought to answer in going to the fountainhead — a representative sample of teacher-educating settings in the major regions of the country. We visited setting after setting without finding what we were looking for: integrated programs of teacher education embracing the full range of knowledge and skills necessary to competent, responsible practices. We are not the only ones who have come up short in similar endeavors.

Agreement on Three Strands

There is high agreement on there being three major strands in this integration: the subject matters of schooling represented in the arts and sciences departments of colleges and universities, the pedagogy that embraces these and the multiple intelligences of human development, and the honing of these learnings in practice. For integration to occur, these strands must come together in common mission. That is, they must make a whole — the program of the professional educator who is to put *the good*, the moral, into the education of the young.

What we found were scattered pieces, some of them well shaped into a curricular strand not joined with the other strands to make a whole. The arts and sciences professors were doing their thing of providing general or specialized subject education, not often influenced by the fact that future teachers were in their classes and that what they were studying are basic tools of school teaching. Even many of the courses in the schools of education that were required for future teachers addressed the subject matter with little attention to its implications for pedagogy. Teachers in cooperating schools received the neophytes into their classrooms without knowing much about what these student teachers were doing in the university-delivered portion of their preparation. We found little evidence of these three groups joining in the sustained conversation necessary to the development of coherent, renewing, whole programs.

We probed deeply into the content of these disparate pieces, hoping to find some commonness of mission that might be tying them together in the necessary wholeness in spite of this absence of collaboration. We found two settings where there was some serious effort to develop in future teachers understanding of their role in enculturating the young into a social and political democracy. The students we interviewed in all the settings thought that this might be a good thing to do but could remember little to nothing in their classes that addressed such. Most of the professors liked the idea but admitted that they were not addressing it.

An Apprenticeship in Democracy

Two decades of inquiry — some of it in close association with schools and teacher-preparing institutions over several years, most of it employing both quantitative and qualitative methods of research — led overwhelmingly to the conclusion that our system of schooling does not deliberately and consciously provide the apprenticeship in democracy necessary to responsible citizenship. Clearly, some schools are providing, thanks to the awareness and dedication of responsible teachers, the attention to the personal and associational development of the young that most parents believe they should. This probably is part of the reason why polls show high public ratings of teachers and of schools people know, even while our political and corporate leaders of school reform declare schooling to be a disaster.

We pondered the general absence — in schooling, individual schools, and educator preparation programs — of infrastructures of educational renewal. Largely absent were scheduled conversations about overall programmatic aims, strengths, and weaknesses, let alone ongoing processes of making decisions, taking action, and evaluating consequences. The ethos of schooling and school reform is that of doing better what the longstanding, deep structure of the enterprise ordains. Following eras of mandated reform, the institutions concentrate on getting back to where they think they were before. Agendas designed for innovation and fundamental change must provide mission, identification of conditions to be put in place, and guidelines for the necessary change strategies and their support.

This is the realization that came to Ken, Roger, and me as we progressed with the study of the education of educators and the writing of the trilogy that culminated it. The Agenda for Education in a Democracy that we developed first appeared in *Teachers for Our Nation's Schools*, a book of the trilogy published in 1990. More flesh was put on its framework in a book published four years later, but nothing was changed.[12] Feedback from the 14 years of "proofing" that have occurred since the Agenda's initial formulation has led to further refinement but no basic revisions.

As the Agenda began to take shape in our minds, we became increasingly aware that simply putting it into the public domain would be less than satisfying. In collaboration with the Education Commission of the States and the American Association of Colleges for Teacher Education, we spread the word that we were seeking a few settings interested in forming school-university partnerships for institutional and programmatic renewal guided by a mission of preparing teachers and teacher educators for educating the young in democratic citizenship. Clearly, we were not alone in sensing the need for such an agenda. We received more than 200 inquiries, most of them appearing to be serious. We decided to proceed with eight settings and developed a selection process of reading and conversation in which more than 50 settings engaged over a period of several months and then submitted formal applications.

The resulting National Network for Educational Renewal (NNER) grew rather quickly to 16 settings, to which it was deliberately held for several years of quality building.[13] It has since slowly expanded to 23 school-university partnerships in 20 states, embracing a diverse group of 40 colleges and universities, more than 100 school districts, and some 800 professional development schools referred to as partner schools. The Agenda for Education in a Democracy provides the mantra for the educational renewal to which all settings are committed.

Created in the early 1990s, the Institute for Educational Inquiry (IEI) in Seattle has provided technical support, secured philanthropic funding for an array of focused initiatives in NNER settings, facilitated networking, trained teams of onsite leaders for advancing the Agenda, and produced a steady flow of papers and books on its component elements, concepts, and principles. A book published in 2004, *Education for Everyone: Agenda for Education in a Democracy*, seeks to provide in short space an introduction to the whole, from mission to strategies of implementation, for participants, educators beyond the NNER, and interested citizens.[14] Our hope is that this publication will encourage readers to dig more deeply by seeking greater understanding of the relationship between education and democracy in the many references cited. There is not space here for detailing the substance of the Agenda.

When I lay before audiences the full story of our educational odyssey — the stages of which have involved both new and continuing colleagues — and the lessons learned, many listeners express concern over what they perceive to be depressing pessimism and realism. To be simultaneously both educator and pessimist is an oxymoron. Most school reform eras have been ushered in with placards and buoyant invitations to get on the train even though we do not know where it is going or how well equipped it is to carry us to destinations not yet determined. What most of these have accomplished through their repeated failures is to convince many people that it is schooling, not the reforms and their political and business leaders, that have failed us.

It is both realistic and wise to study these failures for lessons about how to proceed differently. At the same time, it is both realistic and wise to study how educators and their institutions conduct business in order for us to learn something about why the fundamental changes many of us believe are necessary simply do not occur, even when we often enter into them with great enthusiasm. When the current era of school reform, mandated by the No Child Left Behind Act, ends — the most ill-conceived era of all time — we still will be faced with a system of schooling that is out of sync with the need to prepare the young for satisfying, responsible citizenship in a democracy; with what we know about cognition and other characteristics of human development; and with the learning necessary for wending one's way successfully through the exigencies of our changing world.

There is now a stirring in this land that calls for our rising to a higher plane, a call that might readily be interpreted as seeking commitment to the full range of associational dispositions embedded in the word *democracy*. Nothing would be more uplifting for teaching as a profession and more compelling for those engaged in it or attracted to it than for our schools and educator-preparing programs to be called on to provide for the nation's young an apprenticeship of democracy. Of course the agenda is daunting. If it were not, it would be in place already. The time has come for us to answer the call in time to fend off the eduviruses of eras of school reform yet to come.

Notes

1. *The People Shall Judge*, edited by the staff, Social Sciences 1, The College of the University of Chicago (Chicago: University of Chicago Press, 1949), p. vii.
2. David Brooks, "Arguing with Oakeshott," *The New York Times,* 23 December 2003, p. A35.
3. Wendell Berry, *In the Presence of Fear* (Great Barrington, Mass.: The Orion Society, 2001), p. 6.
4. Kenneth A. Sirotnik, "Society, Schooling, Teaching, and Preparing to Teach," in *The Moral Dimensions of Teaching*, edited by John I. Goodlad, Roger Soder, and Kenneth A. Sirotnik (San Francisco: Jossey-Bass, 1990), p. 307.
5. Johannes Althusius, *Politica*, edited and translated by F.S. Carney (Indianapolis: Liberty Press, 1995), p. 7. Original work published 1603 and 1614.

6. See my *In Praise of Education* (New York: Teachers College Press, 1997), especially Chapter Two; and "Convergence" in *Developing Democratic Character in the Young*, edited by Roger Soder, John I. Goodlad, and Timothy J. McMannon (San Francisco: Jossey-Bass, 2001), pp. 1-25.

7. For more on what appears to have been a very contemporary struggle over the purposes of schooling in China eight centuries ago, see Wm. Theodore de Bary and John W. Chaffee, eds., *Neo-Confucian Education: The Formative Stage* (Berkeley: University of California Press, 1989).

8. Benjamin R. Barber, "Public Schooling: Education for Democracy," in *The Public Purpose of Education and Schooling*, edited by John I. Goodlad and Timothy J. McMannon (San Francisco: Jossey-Bass, 1997), p. 26.

9. See, for example, the amount of public agreement on these found in the chapters titled "We Want It All" in Ernest L. Boyer, *High School* (New York: Harper & Row, 1983), and John I. Goodlad, *A Place Called School*, 20th Anniversary Edition (New York: McGraw-Hill, 2004).

10. John I. Goodlad, *Teachers for Our Nation's Schools*; John I. Goodlad, Roger Soder, and Kenneth A. Sirotnik, eds., *Places Where Teachers Are Taught* and *The Moral Dimensions of Teaching* (San Francisco: Jossey-Bass, 1990).

11. Roger Soder, John I. Goodlad, and Timothy J. McMannon, eds., *Developing Democratic Character in the Young* (San Francisco: Jossey-Bass, 2001).

12. John I. Goodlad, *Educational Renewal: Better Teachers, Better Schools* (San Francisco: Jossey-Bass, 1994).

13. For an account of the work in which these settings engaged for the first ten years and lessons learned from their experiences with the Agenda, see Kenneth A. Sirotnik and Associates, *Renewing Schools & Teacher Education: An Odyssey in Educational Change* (Washington, D.C.: American Association of Colleges for Teacher Education, 2001).

14. John I. Goodlad, Corinne Mantle-Bromley, and Stephen J. Goodlad, *Education for Everyone: Agenda for Education in a Democracy* (San Francisco: Jossey-Bass, 2004).

PUBLIC EDUCATION IS THE COMMON WEALTH OF THE NATION

M. DONALD THOMAS AND JOAN P. KOWAL

Every good and excellent thing stands moment by moment on a razor edge of danger and must be fought for.
— Thornton Wilder

In *My Declaration of Independence,* Senator James M. Jeffords of Vermont wrote that he had many differences with the domestic policies of President George W. Bush:

> The largest for me is education. I come from the state of Justin Smith Morrill, a U.S. Senator who gave America the land grant college systems. His Republican Party stood for opportunity for all, for opening the doors of public school education for every American child. Now, for some, success seems to be measured by the number of students moved out of public schools. (Jeffords 2001, p. 6)

Fred Hechinger, a highly respected education writer, stated it even more forcefully:

M. Donald Thomas is currently a principal with H. Dale Holden and Associates, a South Carolina-based international consulting firm. He has served as superintendent of schools in Salt Lake City and as a consultant to governors in South Carolina, Tennessee, and South Dakota. Joan P. Kowal is Superintendent in Residence/Program Professor at NOVA Southeastern University. She has served in four urban superintendencies over the last 15 of her 34 years in public education.

> America is in headlong retreat from its commitment to education. Political confusion and economic uncertainty have shaken the people's faith in education as the key to financial and social success . . . at stake is nothing less than the survival of American democracy. (Thomas 1981, p. 7)

The United States of America is like a cluster of grapes. The individual grapes are held together by a common stem. The grapes may differ in color, shape, or size. However, each has the strength of the whole. For the United States, the stem is public education.

This simile may be too simple for some. Nevertheless, it illustrates how our nation functions. Individual men and women, different in many ways, are bonded together by a common public education. Common education is the glue that gives us a sense of well-being in the knowledge that we are secure and guaranteed the exercise of personal liberties. Public education establishes a common core of values that defend, protect, appreciate, and extend democracy.

What needs to be recognized is that the American experiment was based on something. It did not just happen. Those who founded this nation wrote important ideas into our national documents. These ideas must be taught in our schools. The ideas form an ethos that supports diversity, a common language with the freedom to learn any other language one wishes or needs to learn, personal freedom, and collective security. These ideas are a set of political principles that separate us as a democratic nation from other, particularly nondemocratic, nations. The ethos embodies intellectual thought that establishes freedom, justice, orderly processes, equal opportunity for all, and a free system of public education, which W.E.B. Du Bois called "the most fundamental" of our civil rights.

Our fundamental principles were established against a background of abuse, exploitation, and political repression. American values have withstood the test of a civil war, assassinations of national leaders, economic depressions, corruption in high places, explosive growth, the agonies of the Vietnam War, adjustment to scarcity, and attacks by internal and external terrorists. The system has worked well.

In some circles it has now become fashionable to claim that democracy has not solved all of our problems nor worked effectively for everyone. The extremes of a democratic society have no easy solutions. The diversity and complexity of our political system is incongruent with simple processes. Unresolved problems may be the penalty we pay for political democracy, personal liberties, and the right to learn.

What is important, however, is that the American ethos, learned in our schools, has been the social bond that has held us together. That ethos has been expressed in many ways by our teachers: fundamental assumptions, ethical principles, national beliefs, political and economic principles, fundamental rights, common moral values, Western traditions, and democratic ideas. Call it what you will, our schools have taught us that the American ethos consists of at least the following:

1. Belief in the worth and the perfectibility of human life.
2. Conviction that democratic societies have more to offer than totalitarian ones.
3. Faith in reason and orderly, peaceful solutions to conflicts between individuals and nations.
4. Respect for knowledge and a strong commitment to education for all.
5. Protection of personal liberties within limits established by law.
6. Equal protection under the law and equal opportunity for personal and economic success.

The pre-eminence of public education as the basis for the common good and the safeguard of democracy was well stated by Elie Wiesel, the Nobel Peace Prize winner in 1986. He asked a group of graduates, and all of us, to think about what education really means. Hearing the responses, he said, "In other words, education must, almost by definition, bring people together, bring generations together. . . . True education negates fanaticism" (quoted in *Parade Magazine*, 24 May 1992).

Similar sentiments are expressed by A.M. Schlesinger in *The Disuniting of America*:

> Our task is to combine due appreciation of the splendid diversity of the nation with due emphasis on the great unifying Western ideas of individual freedom, political democracy and human rights. The American Experience is based on common ideals, common political institutions, common language, common culture, common fate that holds the republic together. (1991, p. 138)

Schlesinger is not alone in his belief that the "commonwealth" as the foundation of democratic societies is fueled by public education. The principle of *E pluribus unum* that forged a new nation on a new continent also was well articulated by David Gergen, who said, "What has made us special in history is that we have tried so hard — and spilled so much blood — to make equal justice and equal opportunity a living reality, to bring unity from diversity" (quoted in *U.S. News and World Report*, 11 May 1992).

Public education has historically been seen as the engine of our democracy, bringing reality to the philosophical ideas of our founders. This notion has been endlessly reiterated. W.E.B. Du Bois stated that the "right to learn" was the most important of all our civil rights. David Tyack has called public education "the one best system." Horace Mann said, "The public school is the greatest discovery made by man."

But today there are countervailing voices, and they are becoming louder.

Education, But Not for All

Today public education is under attack from extremists who do not wish to educate well all of our children. Their attacks on public education come in several forms:

- Attempts to Christianize public education.
- Attempts to privatize the public schools.
- Inadequate financial support for education.

- Promotion of vouchers for educational choices.
- Falsification of school results to portray public education as inadequate.

These types of attacks merit some scrutiny.

Attempts to Christianize Public Education. Since the beginning of time, religious leaders have tried to control what their believers — and often others — should and should not learn. Learning has in many instances been thereby reduced to fit within narrowly prescribed dogma. Consequently, much evil has been committed in the name of religion — Christian, Muslim, you name it. In the United States we can witness continual attempts by right-wing religious zealots to "Christianize" public education. This use of religion is an attempt on the part of *some* to control what *all* children may and may not learn. Where zealots are successful, there are book-burnings, and children are denied access to "harmful" information — information contrary to the narrow beliefs of the zealots.

Individuals and groups who criticize public schools in this way desire to control the minds of our children and to limit learning to a narrow, distorted set of values that no longer provides the ethos of a democratic society. Such dogma restricts the freedom to think independently, including the freedom to worship as one sees fit. These zealots believe there is only "one true religion" — theirs — and schools must conform.

In reality, we do not live in a society where "father (or pastor) knows best" and where our national aim is to conquer the "heathens" and save them for Christ. In truth, we never did live in that mythical realm. But today, the fact that the world is not like the myth is even more strongly in evidence. The world has evolved into one giant society in which not all nations wish to be either democratic or Christian, but in which all nations need to get along for the survival of the planet. The same is true within the United States of America. Our diversity demands free access to information and ideas, regardless of their source. All the safeguards of our democracy, including the freedom to worship as we choose, are strengthened by adherence to the principle of separation of church and state. Nowhere is it more important to uphold that principle than in public education.

Attempts to Privatize the Public Schools. Efforts at privatization are an ill-disguised attempt to weaken public education. Supporters of privatization, simply stated, wish to structure education in order to maintain a supply of minimum-wage workers to support a small elite workforce. These supporters, both individuals and groups, are not interested in providing adequate finances for public education that is designed to meet the learning needs of all children.

Public education privateers are intent on serving their own interests and have little concern for the common good. Many attempts to privatize schools have produced a miserable record of poor results even for those children they purportedly intend to help. The results are no better than those produced by the public schools. Yet, in their rhetoric many supporters of privatization shamelessly distort the facts, claiming to help poor children, for example, when the opposite is true. Privatization of public education is a deliberate effort to control the aims of our free education system. If successful, privatizing public education eventually will undermine the basic fabric of our democratic society. The common good will be traded for private advantage.

Inadequate Financial Support for Education. More than a dozen state supreme courts in recent years have ruled that public education is not adequately funded. The courts can direct legislative bodies to establish standards of adequacy, but they have no power to ensure that adequacy, in fact, is achieved. In almost every state, the various legislatures have ignored the decisions of their state's high court.

Providing effective education for all children cannot be achieved on the cheap. The various court decisions make it clear that the vision of the justices far exceeds that of the legislators when it comes to defining adequate financial support for public education.

The most intense attack on public education — the federal attack — is directly related to the No Child Left Behind Act. Joe Conason, in his book, *Big Lies,* explains that "the education bill he [Bush] negotiated with Senator Edward Kennedy fell far short of the funding he had originally proposed." The same broken promise had been made to Senator James M. Jeffords of Vermont to fund IDEA at 40% of the needed funds. Conason continues, "He [Bush] cut a billion dollars from programs specified in his own bill" (2003, p. 174).

Lack of legislative foresight at both federal and state levels has resulted in inadequate school funding across the nation.

Promotion of Vouchers for Educational Choices. While the courts have ruled that direct aid to private schools (most operated by religious groups) is unconstitutional, opponents of public education have developed a new strategy: vouchers. Vouchers are intended to provide small amounts of public money to parents in order to encourage them to take their children out of the public schools and to place them in private schools. Supporters of vouchers argue that such funding will give poor parents the opportunity to choose the schools best suited to their children's needs, something that wealthy parents have been able to do with their own money.

Ultimately, vouchers will be provided to all parents, wealthy, poor, and in between. The fallacy of the argument is that the value of virtually all proposed vouchers is insufficient to pay the high cost of private education, and poor parents cannot make up the difference. Wealthy parents, of course, will benefit. If they choose private education for their children, they will be able to do so with a partial government subsidy in their pockets.

The voucher system contradicts our democratic principles. It is not, despite rhetoric to the contrary, really for the common good, or the good of all children. Furthermore, vouchers in the case of religion-based schools violate the principle of church-state separation and have the potential for increasing religious conflicts.

Falsification of School Results to Portray Public Education as Inadequate. Individuals and agencies that are frightened by the immense success of public education attempt to discredit our students and our school results by comparing apples to oranges and going bananas over the data. Comparisons of education results among countries that teach and test in different ways are seldom valid. There are too many variables that cannot be controlled:

- Some countries provide preschool education; others do not.
- Some countries provide adequate health care for young children; others do not.
- Some countries have 220 school days each year; others have 180 or fewer.
- Some countries have a longer school day than do other countries.
- Some countries have highly qualified teachers in every classroom; others do not.
- Some countries spend more on education than others do.
- Some countries narrowly focus on academics; others take time to integrate nonacademic activities.

For all of these reasons and many more, international comparisons must be viewed with skepticism. A firmer basis for assessment is to view our own system of education over time. Our public schools have a consistent record of success, both educating our children and preserving our democratic principles. Our schools have created opportunities for millions of our children and have furthered the common good of our nation.

We began this essay with a reference to James M. Jefford's *My Declaration of Independence*. It seems appropriate therefore to close by referring to his concluding questions: "Will we strengthen public education and the ladder of opportunity it provides? Or will we decide through our funding decisions that a high-quality education for all students is not a high federal priority? . . . The American people, I hope, will not stand for it" (2001, p. 136).

Our hope is that this nation will not stand by to witness the possible destruction of our public education system. It is the strongest foundation for an effective democracy, the protector of our common good, and our best hope for a compassionate and just society.

References

Conason, Joe. *Big Lies*. New York: St. Martin's, 2003.

Jeffords, James M. *My Declaration of Independence*. New York: Simon and Shuster, 2001.

Kowal, Joan P., and Thomas, M. Donald. *What's Right with Public Education*. Fastback 501. Bloomington, Ind.: Phi Delta Kappa Educational Foundation, 2002.

Thomas, M. Donald. *Pluralism Gone Mad*. Fastback 160. Bloomington, Ind.: Phi Delta Kappa Educational Foundation, 1981.

Schlesinger, A.M. *The Disuniting of America*. New York: W.W. Norton, 1991.

EDUCATING THE "GOOD" CITIZEN: Political Choices and Pedagogical Goals

JOEL WESTHEIMER AND JOSEPH KAHNE

At the level of rhetoric, most educators, policy makers, and citizens agree that developing students' capacities and commitments for effective and democratic citizenship is important. When we get specific about what democracy requires and about what kind of school curricula will best promote it, however, much of that consensus falls away. For some, a commitment to democracy is a promise to protect liberal notions of freedom, while for others democracy is primarily about equality or equality of opportunity. For some, civil society is the key, while for others, free markets

Joel Westheimer is an associate professor in the social foundations of education at the University of Ottawa, where he directs Democratic Dialogue, a research collaboration for inquiry into democracy, education, and society. Joseph Kahne is the Kathryn P. Hannam Professor of American Studies, a professor of education, and co-director of the Institute for Civic Leadership at Mills College, Oakland, Calif. This essay is reprinted from the April 2004 issue of *PS: Political Science and Politics*. The research was generously supported by the Surdna Foundation with additional support from the Social Sciences and Humanities Research Council of Canada. Parts of this chapter are adapted from a more detailed analysis of our data which appears in the Summer 2004 issue of the *American Educational Research Journal*. The authors wish to thank Harry Boyte, Pamela Burdman, Bernadette Chi, Larry Cuban, Jeff Howard, Gordon Lafer, Barbara Leckie, Bethany Rogers, Robert Sherman, Dorothy Shipps, Jim Toole, and anonymous reviewers. The authors are solely responsible for any and all conclusions. The authors can be reached at joelw@uottawa.ca and jkahne@mills.edu.

are the great hope for a democratic society. For some, good citizens in a democracy volunteer, while for others, they take active parts in political processes by voting, protesting, and working on political campaigns.

It is not surprising, then, that the growing number of educational programs that seek to further democracy by nurturing "good" citizens embody a similarly broad variety of goals and practices. There is a spectrum of ideas about what good citizenship *is* and what good citizens *do* that is embodied by democratic education programs nationwide. There is a narrow and often ideologically conservative conception of citizenship embedded in many current efforts at teaching for democracy that reflects neither arbitrary choices nor pedagogical limitations but rather political choices with political consequences.

Consider, for example, the following perspectives. In 1985, Bill Bennett, then Secretary of Education under Ronald Reagan, wrote: "A democracy depends on schools that help to foster a kind of character which respects the law and . . . respects the value of the individual" (1985).

That same year, in his book *The Politics of Education: Culture, Power and Liberation*, Paulo Freire stated that, "Democracy requires oppressed groups to develop political determination, that is, to organize and mobilize in order to achieve their own objectives. Education can make possible such a democracy" (1985). The next year, Albert Shanker, then president of the American Federation of Teachers, had this to say in a speech titled "Education and Democratic Citizenship": "How can we fail to build a world in which the rights due to every human being from birth are respected? In order to build this world . . . we must [have schools] teach democracy." Finally, President George W. Bush recently established the National Veterans Awareness week and launched a new school program aimed at rekindling our democratic spirit. He called the program "Lessons of Liberty" in which, in the words of the president: "Veterans will visit elementary and high school classrooms to teach the ideals of democracy and freedom that American servicemen have defended for over two centuries" (2001).

Each of these quotations takes seriously the idea that schools are essential for democracy. Yet Bennett, Freire, Shanker, and Bush each provide their own sense of what democracy requires and how schools can help us strengthen their respective — and often competing — visions of a democratic society. When educators, policy makers, politicians, and community activists pursue democracy, they do so in many different ways and toward many different ends.

Students are no more in agreement on what good citizenship means than are teachers, policy makers, or politicians. We asked students in focus groups what it means to be a good citizen. One in an urban California school said: "Someone who's active and stands up for what they believe in. If they know that something's going on that is wrong, they go out and change it." But a student from a different urban California school told us that to be a good citizen, you need to "follow the rules, I guess, as hard as you can, even though you want to break them sometimes. Like cattle" (Kahne et al. 2003).

For many educators, making the case for democracy and the important role schools have in pursuing it is not difficult. Political scientists and civic educators alike are familiar with statistics documenting a precipitous decline in voting rates, with the biggest declines among young people. Political participation, such as working for a political party, for example, is at a 40-year low (Saguaro Seminar 2000). And targeting what people do not know about civics remains a favorite pastime of not only Jay Leno, but also of educators and politicians. One study, by the National Constitution Center, found that only 38% of respondents could name all three branches of government, while a separate poll conducted two years earlier found that 59% of all Americans could name the three stooges (Dudley and Gitelson 2002). Recent debates about domestic security, individual liberties, and foreign policy have further spurred educators to reexamine the role of schools in educating students to be thoughtful and engaged citizens.

One of the biggest areas of growth has been in the area of service learning and community service. Such practices have been marketed in large part through claims that they can respond to the civic mission of schools. Cities such as Chicago, Washington, D.C., and Atlanta, as well as the entire state of Maryland, have created service and service learning requirements to advance such goals. Indeed, a recent survey by the National Center for Education Statistics revealed that 83% of high schools currently offer community-service opportunities, compared with 27% in 1984. The visions of citizenship reflected in these and related civic education policies and programs warrant careful attention.

Three Kinds of Citizens

What kind of citizen do we need to support an effective democratic society? We examined 10 programs engaged in the Surdna Foundation's Democratic Values Initiative, as part of a multi-year study of school-based programs that aim to teach democratic citizenship. From the study of both democratic theory and program goals and practices, we constructed a framework to order some of the diverse perspectives. We found three visions of "citizenship" particularly helpful: the *personally responsible citizen*; the *participatory citizen*; and the *justice-oriented citizen* (see Table 1).[1]

The Personally Responsible Citizen. The personally responsible citizen acts responsibly in his or her community by, for example, picking up litter, giving blood, recycling, volunteering, and staying out of debt. The personally responsible citizen works and pays taxes, obeys laws, and helps those in need during crises such as snowstorms or floods. The personally responsible citizen contributes to food or clothing drives when asked and volunteers to help those less fortunate whether in a soup kitchen or a senior center. She or he might contribute time, money, or both to charitable causes.

Both those in the character education movement and many of those who advocate community service would emphasize this individualistic vision of good citizenship. Programs that seek to develop personally responsible citizens hope to build character and personal responsibility by emphasizing honesty, integrity, self-discipline, and hard work (Mann 1838; and currently proponents such as Lickona 1993; Wynne 1986). The Character Counts! Coalition, for example, advocates teaching students to "treat others with respect . . . deal peacefully with anger . . . be considerate of the feelings of others . . . follow the Golden Rule . . . use good manners" and so on. They want students not to "threaten, hit, or hurt anyone [or use] bad language" (Character Counts! 1996). Other programs that seek to develop personally responsible citizens hope to nurture compassion by engaging students in volunteer activities. As illustrated in the mission of the Points of Light Foundation, these programs hope to "help solve serious social problems" by "engag[ing] more people more effectively in volunteer service" (Points of Light 2003).

The Participatory Citizen. Other educators see good citizens as those who actively participate in the civic affairs and the social life of the community at local, state, and national levels. We call this kind of citizen the participatory citizen. Educational programs designed to support the development of participatory citizens focus on teaching students about how government and other institutions (e.g., community based organizations, churches) work and about the importance of planning and participating in organized efforts to care for those in need, for example, or in efforts to guide school policies. While the personally responsible citizen would contribute cans of food for the homeless, the participatory citizen might organize the food drive.

In the tradition of Tocqueville, proponents of participatory citizenship argue that civic participation transcends particular community problems or opportunities. It also develops relationships, common understandings, trust, and collective commitments. This perspective, like Benjamin Barber's notion of "strong democracy," adopts a broad notion of the political sphere — one in which citizens "with competing but overlapping interests can contrive to live together communally" (1984, p. 118).

The Justice-Oriented Citizen. A third image of a good citizen is, perhaps, the perspective that is least commonly pursued. We

Table 1. Kinds of citizens.*

	Personally Responsible Citizen	Participatory Citizen	Justice-Oriented Citizen
Description	Acts responsibly in his/her community. Works and pays taxes. Obeys laws. Recycles, gives blood. Volunteers to lend a hand in times of crisis.	Active member of community organizations and/or improvement efforts. Organizes community efforts to care for those in need, promotes economic development, or cleans up environment. Knows how government agencies work. Knows strategies for accomplishing collective tasks.	Critically assesses social, political, and economic structures to see beyond surface causes. Seeks out and addresses areas of injustice. Knows about social movements and how to effect systemic change.
Sample Act	Contributes food to a food drive.	Helps to organize a food drive.	Explores why people are hungry and acts to solve root causes.
Core Assumption	To solve social problems and improve society, citizens must have good character; they must be honest, responsible, and law-abiding members of the community.	To solve social problems and improve society, citizens must actively participate and take leadership positions within established systems and community structures.	To solve social problems and improve society, citizens must question and change established systems and structures when they reproduce patterns of injustice over time.

*We are indebted to James Toole and a focus group of Minnesota teachers for help in structuring this table.

refer to this view as the justice-oriented citizen, one that calls explicit attention to matters of injustice and to the importance of pursuing social justice goals. Justice-oriented citizens critically assess social, political, and economic structures and consider collective strategies for change that challenge injustice and, when possible, address root causes of problems. The vision of the justice-oriented citizen shares with the vision of the participatory citizen an emphasis on collective work related to the life and issues of the community. However, these programs emphasize preparing students to improve society by critically analyzing and addressing social issues and injustices. These programs are less likely to emphasize the need for charity and volunteerism as ends in themselves and more likely to teach about social movements and how to affect systemic change (see, for example, Isaac 1992; Bigelow and Diamond 1988). In other words, if participatory citizens are organizing the food drive and personally responsible citizens are donating food, justice-oriented citizens are asking why people are hungry and acting on what they discover. That today's citizens are "bowling alone" (Putnam 2000) would worry those focused on civic participation. Those who emphasize social justice, however, would worry more that when citizens do get together, they often fail to focus on or to critically analyze the social, economic, and political structures that generate problems. To say this is not to say that justice-oriented citizens necessarily promote a left-of-center perspective. One can adopt a structural approach to "stemming the erosion of support for 'traditional' families" or to "building greater support for 'non-traditional' families," for example.

The strongest proponents of the justice-oriented perspective were likely the Social Reconstructionists who gained their greatest hearing between the two world wars. Educators such as Harold Rugg (1921) argued that the teaching of history in particular and the school curriculum more generally should be developed in ways that connect with important and enduring social problems. Similarly, George Counts wanted educators to critically assess varied social and economic institutions while also "engag[ing] in the positive task of creating a new tradition in American life" (1932). These educators emphasized that truly effective citizens needed opportunities to analyze and understand the interplay of social, economic, and political forces and to take part in projects through which they might develop skills and commitments for working collectively to improve society.[2]

Conflicting Priorities

Is it possible to pursue all three of these visions? Perhaps. Might there be conflicts? Yes. Certainly participatory citizens or those committed to justice can simultaneously be dependable or honest. However, there may also be conflicts. The emphasis placed on individual character and behavior, for example, can obscure the need for collective and often public-sector initiatives.

A vast majority of school-based service learning and community service programs embrace a vision of citizenship devoid of politics; they often promote service but not democracy. They share an orientation toward volunteerism and charity and away from teaching about social movements, social transformation, and systemic change. These programs privilege individual acts of compassion and kindness over social action and the pursuit of social justice.

We find the emphasis placed on personal responsibility and character an inadequate response to the challenges of educating a democratic citizenry. Clearly, personal responsibility traits commonly associated with character (telling the truth, helping others, being polite) may strengthen a democracy by fostering social trust and willingness to commit to collective efforts, for example. We are not arguing against these goals (with the exception of certain visions of obedience that are sometimes associated with this agenda). Our point is rather that granting primacy to this goal can impede other fundamentally important goals for civic educators. Specifically, the emphasis placed on individual character and behavior can obscure the need for collective and often public-sector initiatives; this emphasis can distract attention from analysis of the causes of social problems; and third, volunteerism and kindness are put forward as ways of avoiding politics and policy.

As a way of illustrating what we see as the limitations of personally responsible citizenship, recall the central tenets of the Character Counts! Coalition. Certainly honesty, integrity, and responsibility for one's actions are valuable character traits for good neighbors and citizens. (One might even argue that citizens' sense that other citizens are dishonest, irresponsible, and lack common decency will undermine their desire to participate in democratic processes.) Still, on their own, these traits are not inherently about democracy. To the extent that these traits detract from other important democratic priorities, they hinder, rather than make possible, democratic participation and change. For example, a focus on loyalty or obedience (common components of character education as well) work against the kind of critical reflection and action many assume are essential in a democratic society.

Consider Cesar Chavez Day in California. The state appropriated funds for students from across the state to participate in a wide range of community service experiences honoring Chavez. But the request for proposal to receive these monies included the following statement:

> Although marches, religious services, and political advocacy were important aspects of Chavez's work, such activities do not constitute allowable activities under this grant. . . . Prohibited activities include: lobbying, marches, petitions, participating in events or activities that include advocacy legislation or party platforms.

Such statements are common — indeed, all Americorps members are prohibited from doing anything that engages the political system.

Personal responsibility, voluntarism, and character education must be considered in a broader social context or they risk advancing civility or docility instead of democracy. Indeed, government leaders in a totalitarian regime would be as delighted as leaders in a democracy if their young citizens learned the lessons put forward by many of the proponents of personally responsible citizenship: don't do drugs; show up to school; show up to work; give blood; help others during a flood; recycle; pick up litter; clean up a park; treat old people with respect. The leaders of both China and Syria, as well as George W. Bush, would argue that these are desirable traits for people living in a community. But they are not about democratic citizenship.

Federally funded post 9/11 efforts at renewing citizenship have echoed similar themes while also emphasizing narrow visions of patriotism. The Bush Administration, for instance, wants a new role for civic education programs supported by the Corporation for National and Community Service and the new USA Freedom Corps — one tied to patriotism and homeland defense.

Nebraska offers a more far-reaching example. In November 2001, two months after the terrorist attacks on the World Trade Center, Nebraska's State Board of Education specified that high school social studies curriculum should, "include instruction in . . . the benefits and advantages of our government, the dangers of communism and similar ideologies, the duties of citizenship, and appropriate patriotic exercises, that middle-grade instruction should instill a love of country," and that the social studies curriculum should include "exploits and deeds of American heroes, singing patriotic songs, memorizing the Star Spangled Banner and America, and reverence for the flag" (Nebraska State Board of Education 2001). Indeed, 17 states enacted new pledge laws or amended policies in the 2002-2003 legislative session (Piscatelli 2003).

Recent studies of youth reflect this apolitical conception of citizenship as well. A study commissioned by the National Association of Secretaries of State (1999) found that less than 32% of eligible voters between the ages of 18 and 24 voted in the 1996 presidential election (in 1972, the comparable number was 50%), but that a whopping 94% of those aged 15-24 believed that "the most important thing I can do as a citizen is to help others" (also see Sax et al. 1999). In a very real sense, youths seem to be "learning" that citizenship does not require government, politics, or even collective endeavors (see Andolina et al. 2002).

It's not that youth do not care to express their opinions. We need only look at this season's popular television show, *American Idol*. Number of votes cast by young people for the next American idol? More than 24 million.[3] Young people can be motivated to act, but too many school-based programs stifle, rather than stimulate, collective and democratic attitudes and skills.

Strikingly, research and evaluation of educational programs also reflect this conservative and individualistic conception of personally responsible citizenship. Major studies of civic education programs, for example, ask participants whether they feel it is their responsibility to take care of those in need and whether problems of pollution and toxic waste are "everyone's responsibility." They rarely ask questions about corporate responsibility — in what ways industries should be regulated, for example—or about ways government policies can advance or hinder solutions to social problems. Survey questions typically emphasize individual and charitable acts. They ignore important influences such as social movements and government policy on efforts to improve society (Kahne, Westheimer, and Rogers 2000).

The vision promoted by most school-based initiatives and the evaluations that judge their success is one of citizenship without politics — a commitment to service, but not to democracy.

Participatory and Justice-Oriented Goals

Perhaps we are overstating the point. It may be true that the vast bulk of energy going into education for democracy and citizenship does so in a way that avoids political engagement. Alternatively, it may be that the programs that promote personal responsibility or participatory citizenship enhance commitments to the kind of civic engagement that will ultimately strengthen our democracy. Proponents make this argument, but how well does it hold up? We studied exactly this question. A brief description of our findings from two programs will illustrate our point.[4]

Both programs worked with classes of high school students and both initiatives were designed to support the development of democratic and civic understandings and commitments. But their goals and strategies differed. The first aims to develop participatory citizens; the second, justice-oriented ones.

The Madison County Youth Service League (a pseudonym) is located in a suburban, largely white, East Coast community outside of a city of roughly 23,000 people. One Madison County group of students investigated whether citizens in their community would prefer curbside trash pickup that was organized by the county. Another group explored the development of a five-year plan for the fire and rescue department. For each project, students had to collect and analyze data, interact with government agencies, write a report, and present their findings in a formal hearing in front of the county's board of supervisors.

We saw evidence that the Madison County students learned a great deal about micro-politics, such as how different government offices compete for funding. And students talked about the powerful impact of realizing that what they did would or could make a difference. One student told us that before he started the program, he thought it was "just going to be another project [where] we do some research, we leave and it gets put on the shelf somewhere." But he was pleasantly surprised at the extent of the impact their projects had on the community. "We've been in the newspaper," another student noted, "a lot!"

But we found little evidence that the Madison County students learned about broader ideological and political issues related to interest groups and the political process, the causes of poverty, different groups' need for health care, or the fairness of different systems of taxation (even though two projects focused on issues related to health care and taxation). Students focused on particular programs and policies and aimed for "technocratic/value neutral" analysis. Perhaps not surprisingly, our analysis of student interviews indicated that the curriculum did not appear to change students' interest in politics or their perspectives on structural issues related to, for example, possible causes of poverty.

Quantitative results reinforced our findings from observations and interviews. Statistically significant gains were recorded in several important areas, such as in the knowledge and social capital needed for community development and students' sense of civic efficacy — that they could make a difference in their community. Madison County students also increased their scores on our measures of personal responsibility and leadership efficacy. However, the program did not alter students' interest in political engagement.

In the second program, politics took center stage. Bayside Students for Justice is a curriculum developed as part of a social studies course in a large, urban, West Coast high school with a highly diverse student body. This program had goals oriented around improving society through structural changes. As one of the teachers for this program put it, "My goal is to empower [students] to focus on things that they care about in their own lives and to . . . show them avenues that they can use to achieve real social change, profound social change." The program advanced a justice-oriented vision of citizenship.

Some students investigated the lack of access to a local health care center for women. Others sought ways to challenge a Senate bill that would put students and their parents in jail for truancy and would try juveniles as adults for certain crimes. Others studied the social, political, and economic causes and consequences of violence in their community.

Like their Madison County peers, the Bayside students expressed a passion for the real-world connections to their academic studies. But these students appeared to take away different lessons. Our survey results show that Bayside students, to a much greater degree than those from Madison County, learned forms of civic involvement that addressed a macro-level critique of society. And, in interviews, students expressed a strong sense of the need to address these problems collectively, rather than as individuals. One student observed that in most classrooms, "it seems like everyone works as an individual to better themselves, but in this class, we're working as a group to better everything around us."

In comparison to Madison County Youth Service League, the Bayside Students for Justice curriculum appeared to emphasize social critique significantly more and technocratic skills associated with participation somewhat less. To the extent that Bayside students learned about participatory skills, they focused on extra-governmental social activism that challenged, rather than reinforced, existing norms (such as community organizing or protesting). For example, students were more likely at the end of the program than at the beginning to posit structural explanations for social problems (stating, for example, that the problem of poverty resulted from too few jobs that pay wages high enough to support a family, rather than being a result of individuals being lazy and not wanting to work). Survey results also showed that while students who participated in Madison County Youth Service League reported an increased sense of personal responsibility to help others and sizable increases on measures related to active participation, knowledge/ social capital for community development, and leadership efficacy, those in Bayside Students for Justice reported increased interest in politics and political issues and were more likely to seek redress of root causes of difficult social ills. As one student told us after several months in the Bayside program, "when the economy's bad and people start blaming immigrants or whoever else they can blame, they've got to realize that there are big social, economic, and political issues tied together, that it's not the immigrants, no it's bigger than them."

Table 2. Pre/Post changes.

Measures	Madison County Youth Service League (N=61) CHANGE (pre/post)	Bayside Students for Justice (N=21) CHANGE (pre/post)
Personal responsibility to help others	.21* (4.00→4.21)	.09 (3.84→3.93)
Knowledge/social capital for community development	.94** (3.95→4.89)	.17 (2.76→2.93)
Leadership efficacy	.31** (3.60→3.91)	.12 (3.13→3.25)
Interest in politics	.03 (3.41‡→3.44)	.33* (2.68→3.01)
Structural/individual explanations for poverty	-.10 (3.13→3.03)	.28* (3.88→4.16)
Civic efficacy	.34** (3.78→4.12)	.47* (3.03→3.50)
Government responsibility for those in need	.24* (3.10→3.34)	.29* (3.19→3.48)
Vision to help	.30* (2.65→2.95)	.36 (2.43→2.79)

Pre and post surveys were administered to all program participants. For a detailed discussion of these measures and findings, see Westheimer and Kahne 2004.
*p < .05
**p < .01

The Politics of Pursuing Dual Goals

As noted earlier, those committed to educating social activists who practice justice-oriented citizenship would ideally want to couple critical analysis of root causes of injustice with opportunities to develop capacities for participation. They want students to be able to both analyze and understand structural causes of deeply entrenched social problems *and* gain the skills and motivation to act by participating in local and national politics and community forums. But a focus on justice guarantees neither the motivation nor the capacity to participate in democratic change. Many — ourselves included — would applaud programs that manage to emphasize justice-oriented citizenship inextricably linked to a desire and capacity for participation. However, our findings indicate that engaging in critical analysis does not necessarily foster the ability or the commitment to participate. The reverse is also true: Students can learn to participate without engaging in critical analysis that focuses on macro structural issues, the role of interest groups, power dynamics, and/or social justice. The ability to spot injustice is not organically linked to the inclination or the ability to take action.[5]

The relative emphasis placed on these differing goals will likely depend on numerous factors. These include: the structure of the curriculum, the priorities of those designing and implementing the initiative, and the time available for such instruction. Moreover, the political constraints and value-based priorities of both administrators and community members are also likely to affect the structure of the curriculum.

Conclusion

So, what does this mean for teaching democracy? For those of us interested in schooling's civic purposes, we maintain that it is not enough to argue that democratic values are as important as traditional academic priorities. We must also ask what kind of values. What political and ideological interests are embedded in varied conceptions of citizenship?

First, school programs that hope to develop personally responsible citizens may not be effective at increasing participation in local and national civic affairs. In fact, efforts to pursue some conceptions of personal responsibility can undermine efforts to prepare participatory and justice-oriented citizens.

Second, the study of the Madison County Youth Service League and the Bayside Students for Justice demonstrates the importance of distinguishing between programs that emphasize participatory citizenship and those that emphasize the pursuit of justice. While each program was effective in achieving its goals, qualitative and quantitative data regarding these programs demonstrated important differences in each program's impact. Programs that champion participation do not necessarily develop students' abilities to analyze and critique root causes of social problems and vice versa. Although many committed to the democratic purposes of education may extol the value of linking priorities related to participation and justice, our study indicates that this outcome is not guaranteed. If both goals are priorities, those designing and implementing curriculum must give both explicit attention.

Finally, although most current programs are aimed only at personally responsible citizenship, educating for democratic citizenship *is* possible.[6] Those of us who design and teach these curricula and those studying their impact must be aware of different — and at times conflicting — visions of citizenship and their political implications. Democracy is not self-winding. Students need to be taught to participate in our democracy, and different programs aim at different goals. We need to choose carefully. The choices we make have consequences for the kind of society we ultimately help to create.

Notes

1. These three categories were chosen because they satisfied our two main criteria: 1) they aligned well with prominent theoretical perspectives described above, and 2) they articulate ideas and ideals that resonate with practitioners (teachers, administrators, and curriculum designers). To that end, we consulted with both the 10 teams of educators whose work we studied and with other leaders in the field in an effort to create categories and descriptions that aligned well with and communicated clearly their differing priorities. Our desire to respond to prominent educational theories related to democratic ideals and to develop a framework that practitioners would find both clear and meaningful led us to modify our categories in several ways. For example, we began this study emphasizing a distinction between

"charity" and "change." We had used this distinction in earlier writing (Kahne and Westheimer 1996). Through the course of our work, however, it became clear that this distinction did not do enough to capture main currents in dialogues of practitioners and scholars regarding democratic educational goals and ways to achieve them (see also Westheimer and Kahne 2000). In addition, once our three categories were identified, we found that some of our rhetoric failed to clearly convey our intent. For example, we had initially titled our third category the "social reconstructionist." As a result of dialogues with practitioners, this was changed to the "social reformer" and finally to the "justice-oriented citizen." In making these distinctions, we do not mean to imply that a given program might not simultaneously further more than one of these agendas. These categories were not designed to be mutually exclusive. At the same time, we believe that drawing attention to the distinctions between these visions of citizenship is important. It highlights the importance of examining the underlying goals and assumptions that drive different educational programs in design and practice.

2. For a description of a contemporary curriculum that reflects this emphasis, see Westheimer and Kahne 2002.

3. Martha Paskoff, "Idol Worship: What American Politics Can Learn From *American Idol*," *American Prospect Online*, 23 May 2003.

4. For a more detailed report of the study, see Westheimer and Kahne 2004 or contact the authors at joelw@uottawa.ca or jkahne@mills.edu.

5. For a related study see Kahne, Chi, and Middaugh 2003.

6. See Joseph Kahne and Joel Westheimer, "Teaching Democracy: What Schools Need to Do," *Phi Delta Kappan* (September 2003) for an exploration of the strategies effective programs use to teach for democratic citizenship.

References

Andolina, Molly; Jenkins, Krista; Keeter, Scott; and Zukin, Cliff. "Searching for the Meaning of Youth Civic Engagement: Notes from the Field." *Applied Developmental Science* 6, no. 4 (2002): 189-95.

Barber, Benjamin. *Strong Democracy: Participatory Politics for a New Age*. Berkeley: University of California Press, 1984.

Bennett, William J. "Education for Democracy." Paper presented at the regular meeting of the *Consejo Interamericano para la Education, la Ciencia, y la Cultura*. Washington, D.C., 1985.

Bigelow, William, and Diamond, Norman. *The Power in Our Hands: A Curriculum on the History of Work and Workers in the United States.* New York: Monthly Review Press, 1988.

Bush, George W. "President Bush Launches Effort to Bring Students and Veterans Together in America's Classrooms: Education and Veterans Affairs Team Up to Promote 'Lessons of Liberty'." U.S. Department of Education press release, 30 October 2001. www.ed. gov/PressReleases/ 10-2001/10302001.html

Character Counts! *Character Counts.* Los Angeles, 1996.

Dudley, Robert L., and Gitelson, Alan R. "Political Literacy, Civic Education, and Civic Engagement: A Return to Political Socialization?" *Applied Developmental Science* 6, no. 4 (2002): 175-82.

Freire, Paulo. *The Politics of Education: Culture, Power and Liberation.* South Hadley, Mass.: Bergin & Garvey, 1985.

Isaac, Katherine. *Civics for Democracy: The Journey for Teachers and Students.* Washington, D.C.: Essential Books, 1992.

Kahne, Joseph; Chi, Bernadette; and Middaugh, Ellen. "Democratic Education: The Untapped Potential of High School Government Courses." Under review. 2003. Please contact jkahne@mills.edu for copies.

Kahne, Joseph, and Westheimer, Joel. "Teaching Democracy: What Schools Need to Do." *Phi Delta Kappan* 85 (September 2003): 34-40, 57-66.

Kahne, Joseph, and Westheimer, Joel. "In the Service of What? The Politics of Service Learning." *Phi Delta Kappan* 77 (May 1996): 593-99.

Kahne, Joseph; Westheimer, Joel; and Rogers, Bethany. "Service Learning and Citizenship in Higher Education." *Michigan Journal of Community Service Learning* (Fall 2000): 42-51.

Lickona, Thomas. "The Return of Character Education." *Educational Leadership* 51, no. 3 (1993): 6-11.

Mann, Horace. *First Annual Report.* Boston: Dutton & Wentworth, 1838.

National Association of Secretaries of State. *New Millennium Project-Phase I: A Nationwide Study of 15-24 Year Old Youth.* Alexandria, Va.: Tarrance Group, 1999.

Nebraska State Board of Education, "Board Minutes, 1-2 Nov. 2001." (Revised following 7 Dec. meeting).

Piscatelli, Jennifer. "Pledge of Allegiance." *State Notes: Character and Civic Education. Education Commission of the States.* (August 2003).

Points of Light Foundation website. 2003. http://www.pointsoflight.org.

Putnam, Robert D. *Bowling Alone: The Collapse and Revival of American Community.* New York: Simon & Schuster, 2000.

Rugg, Harold O. "Reconstructing the Curriculum: An Open Letter to Professor Henry Johnson Commenting on Committee Procedure as Illustrated by the Report of the Joint Committee on History and Education for Citizenship." *Historical Outlook* 12 (1921): 184-89. Reprinted in Parker, W.C., ed. *Educating the Democratic Mind.* Albany: State University of New York Press, 1996.

Saguaro Seminar. *Report of the Saguaro Seminar: Civic Engagement.* Boston, 2000.

Sax, Linda J.; Astin, Alexander; Korn, William S.; and Mahoney, Kathryn M. *The American Freshman: National Norms for Fall 1999.* Los Angeles: Higher Education Research Institute, UCLA, 1999.

Shanker, Albert. "Education and Democratic Citizenship." Speech to the 1986 meeting of the American Federation of Teachers, as quoted in Shanker, A. "Education and Democratic Citizenship: Where We Stand." *International Journal of Social Education* 12 (1997): 1-10.

Westheimer, Joel, and Kahne, Joseph. "Educating for Democracy." In *Democracy's Moment: Reforming the American Political System for the 21st Century,* edited by R. Hayduk and K. Mattson. Lanham, Md.: Rowman & Littlefield, 2002.

Westheimer, Joel, and Kahne, Joseph. "Service Learning Required: But What Exactly Do Students Learn?" *Education Week,* "Commentary," 26 January 2000, p. 42.

Wynne, Ed A. "The Great Tradition in Education: Transmitting Moral Values." *Educational Leadership* 43, no. 4 (1986): 4-9.

THE AMERICAN TRADITION OF EDUCATION

J. MERRELL HANSEN

A petition circulated in the state legislature of the Common-wealth of Massachusetts Bay in 1787. The country was still young; and the concepts of democracy, citizenship, and national identity still were being formed. These petitioners saw a critical need and sought the attention of those who governed.

> We are of the humble opinion that we have the right to enjoy the privileges of free men. But that we do not will appear in many instances, and we beg leave to mention one out of many, and that is the education of our children which now receive no benefit from the free schools in the town of Boston, which we think is a great grievance, as by woful experience we now feel the want of a common education. We, therefore, must fear for our rising offspring to see them in ignorance in a land of gospel light when there is provision made for them as well as others and yet can't enjoy them, and for no other reason can be given this they are black. . . . We therefore pray your Honors that you would in your wis-

J. Merrell Hansen is a professor of education at Brigham Young University. Hansen received his Ph.D. from the University of Texas at Austin in 1971 and has taught at the University of Kentucky and Washington State University. His research interests include the foundations of education, teacher education, and social studies education.

dom some provision might be made for the free education of our dear children. And in duty bound shall ever pray. (Hakim 2003, p. 1)

These individuals were pleading for free and universal public education, not education just for the privileged classes. They shared a hope that schooling would be available to all individuals regardless of race, national origin, or wealth. This conviction has emerged and re-emerged throughout our history. It seems that whenever there is a crisis, invariably we turn to the one institution that seems the best capable of helping us deal with our problems.

This optimism for public schools began in the Age of Enlightenment. The belief was that good individuals working together, even with disagreements, could ultimately achieve their goals without war and bloodshed. However, this would not occur without an enlightened and informed citizenry. Such a citizenry would arise when education became a national priority and found a permanent place on the political and social agenda.

> In the eighteenth century we developed our ideas about inductive science, about religious and political freedom, about popular education, about rational commerce, and about the nation-state. In the eighteenth century we also invented the idea of progress and, you may be surprised to know, our modern idea of happiness. It was during the eighteenth century that reason began to triumph over superstition. (Postman 1999, pp. 17-18)

There were those who thought that these ideas were too ambitious and that entrusting too much power and influence to citizens would lead to anarchy. This argument is best exemplified by the debate between Alexander Hamilton and Thomas Jefferson (Darling-Hammond 1997). Hamilton was suspicious of the capabilities and values of the common people. Hamilton's lack of faith in the ability of the people to make sound decisions about their own lives and those of their communities — a lack of faith that was shared widely both then and now — was the basis for proposals that this new nation should be governed by elites on behalf of the people, who could not be trusted to govern themselves (Darling-Hammond 1997, p. 41). Jefferson believed that democracy could not survive without an informed and enlightened citizenry.

Such optimistic hopes for democracy depended entirely on the nature and quality of the education provided to every citizen. Thus public education has been and will remain a central part of the national discourse. Without education, we run the obvious risk of regression and degeneration. If humans are capable of self-governance, then schools serve a greater purpose than just instilling particular skills. Schools have a higher purpose. Paraphrasing Jefferson, Commager writes:

> The first duty laid on them was to provide an enlightened citizenry in order that self-government might work. This was a basic tenet of Jeffersonian philosophy, and it has remained basic to American politics as to American educational philosophy. Democracy, to be effective, required an enlightened citizenry. To expect an ignorant or an indifferent electorate to govern themselves wisely was to expect the impossible. (Commager 1976, p. 11)

A number of forces have made the pursuit of high-quality education imperative. These forces include waves of immigration and the change of the workforce from agrarian to industrial to technological to informational. But it should be remembered that public schools were established to promote not just economic freedom, but also intellectual, social, and political freedom. That sometimes is forgotten today. Goodlad writes, "the function of schools today appears to be more to sort the young for their place in society than to educate them for productive, responsible, satisfying participation in it" (2002, p. 18).

Critics often characterize public schools as failing our society and placing the "nation at risk." They propose vouchers, tax credits, alternative choices, and privatization of public schools. While no one would wish to deny "parental choice" or advocate that any child be left behind, we need to understand the motives and intentions of such efforts.

No institution has been asked to do more for our nation than have the public schools. The critics and the cynics claim that we have not done enough, that we have failed. Nevertheless, the public good still is served best by the neighborhood school. Public schools often are the institution closest to the public. And parents consistently regard their local schools "with high regard" (Rose and Gallup 2003, p. 42). They continue to send their children daily to these schools.

The schools are entrusted with a tremendous human and civic responsibility. Our nation is always one generation away from losing a form of government that has taken centuries to develop. If the young do not learn about citizenship and the public good, they will not be prepared for their roles as worthwhile citizens. The next generation needs to understand and to desire freedom, liberty, choices, responsibilities, integrity, and democracy. That is a substantial part of what schools are all about. This needs to be part of the curriculum.

However, civic education is more than learning the facts about government. It also should instill the values and principles that make democracy work. This kind of civic education would have three parts: 1) education *about* democracy, 2) education *for* democratic and civic responsibilities, and 3) education *through* democratic practices.

In the past, we have assumed that students would move toward good citizenship and public participation if we simply taught them about our government. This has not been sufficient. We need to teach *for* democracy. We must develop democratic values in our students. Furthermore, we should help students to practice democracy in their lives.

Our schools should be guided by such practices as justice, fairness, liberty, honesty, equity, and respect for differences. These are demonstrated in how we teach, how we behave, and what we do in our classrooms and schools. That is, we must create schools that exemplify democratic understandings.

We have come a long way in respecting individuals and differences, but bullying and intimidation at school still occur. As society is governed by the principle of "equal protection under the law," so the classroom and school should be places where the individual is secure. Schools that are hurtful and painful should be reformed.

Schools should be places where individual voices are heard. Students who are ignored cease to participate. This invitation to participate should extend beyond the classroom to schoolwide issues. For example, school elections usually are not models of democracy, but popularity contests. A true democracy is decided by voices that understand issues and problems and wish to make a meaningful difference in their resolution. Good citizenship means extending oneself to serve and to contribute.

Schools need to build emotional, social, and intellectual communities. They should be places where students want to be. Schools can become more democratic by fostering a community that respects the individual while encouraging the collective good. It is a place where citizens make decisions, affect policy and practices, show respect for their community and associates, and make a difference in how things are done.

Educators have a moral purpose in what they do. They have both an obligation and an opportunity to teach and to learn in a place that affects our nation's destiny. Educators must teach so that students know the difference between right and wrong and will choose not to live in a world that is wrong. The public good still depends on the public schools and the education they provide to our future citizens.

References

Commager, Henry Steele. *The People and Their Schools*. Fastback 79. Bloomington, Ind.: Phi Delta Kappa Educational Foundation, 1976.

Darling-Hammond, Linda. "Education, Equity, and the Right to Learn." In *The Public Purpose of Education and Schooling*, edited by John I. Goodlad and Timothy J. McMannon. San Francisco: Jossey-Bass, 1997.

Goodlad, John I. "Kudzu, Rabbits, and School Reform." *Phi Delta Kappan* 84 (September 2002): 16-23.

Hakim, Joy. *Freedom: A History of US*. New York: Oxford University Press, 2003.

Postman, Neil. *Building a Bridge to the Eighteenth Century*. New York: Alfred A. Knopf, 1999.

Rose, Lowell C., and Gallup, Alec M. "The 35th Annual Phi Delta Kappa/Gallup Poll of the Public's Attitudes Toward the Public Schools." *Phi Delta Kappan* 85 (September 2003): 41-56.

EIGHT CONSIDERATIONS IN THE BATTLE FOR PUBLIC SCHOOLS

BRUCE M. MITCHELL

Although public education is well-established in the United States, probably at no time in history has it been under such attack. Influential critics of public education emerged soon after World War II. Admiral Hyman Rickover chastised the public schools for not teaching math and science effectively. Rudolph Flesch railed against the public schools for not teaching reading properly. Maxwell Rafferty, the right-leaning Superintendent of Schools in California, chastised the schools for being negligent in phonics instruction. In fact, at one time he even advocated that the schools return to using McGuffey's readers.

In 1954 the *Brown* v. *Board of Education* decision created new dissatisfactions with public schools, particularly in the segregated South. Affluent parents withdrew their children from the newly integrated public schools and enrolled them in segregated private schools. Soon there were a number of ploys designed to acquire public funding for these private schools, but such funding was declared unconstitutional by the courts. This further angered

Bruce M. Mitchell is the co-director and co-founder of Satori Camps for the Gifted/Talented at Eastern Washington University, where he was a professor for 33 years. Mitchell also has been an elementary teacher and principal. His most recent book is *Unequal Education: A Crisis in America's Schools?* (Bergin & Garvey, 2002).

many parents who wanted to maintain their racially segregated schools.

The 1980s brought even more difficulties for public education. President Reagan's call for less government and the privatization of many government functions led many people to view "government controlled" schools with suspicion.

Another source of the new president's dissatisfaction centered on the secretary of education as a cabinet post. That cabinet position was created during the Carter Administration. Reagan appointed T.H. Bell as the first secretary of education in the hope that Bell would help abolish the post. However, Bell became convinced that the office needed to remain a cabinet position, rather than return to the original position in the Department of Health, Education and Welfare; and he was able to persuade Reagan that education should remain as a cabinet position.

During Bell's tenure, a national commission was appointed to study the effectiveness of U.S. public education. The commission's report, *A Nation at Risk*, was a scathing indictment of the nation's schools and their teachers. However, the report was widely criticized because the committee consisted of only college presidents, business and industry representatives, school administrators, a school board member, an ex-governor, and only one high school teacher. Amazingly, there were no representatives for grades K-8. Also, the report had little to say about the increased number of students in poverty, which had a direct effect on test scores and school performance in general.

Many politicians have clamored to become known as the "education politician," regardless of the office they pursued. Various "reforms" were pursued with euphemistic titles, such as the current fad, "No Child Left Behind." Sadly, many of these education reforms called simply for more homework and more testing. For example, the state of California currently is beleaguered with Standardized Testing and Reporting (STAR) and the California Alternate Performance Assessment (CAPA).

The United States currently is afflicted by a mind-boggling emphasis on testing. These tests require teachers to spend countless hours on test drilling, often at the cost of not teaching higher-level thinking strategies and creative thinking development. These thinking behaviors cannot be measured by machines so they are not included on the various tests used throughout the country. Teachers also cannot spend much time on music, art, social studies, physical education, and any other subject not included in the statewide tests.

It is a school's average scores on such tests that determine whether it is branded a "good" school or a "poor" school. However, the preponderance of education research shows that the main variable in a school's test results is per capita income. Schools with a lot of students from wealthy families score high, while schools with a preponderance of poor students score low. One factor is that many affluent children who live in relatively large, high-scoring school districts tend to stay in the public schools, while affluent students who reside in more heterogeneous communities are more likely to opt for a private school. Low-income parents do not have the option of sending their children to private schools because they simply cannot afford it.

The good news is that public schools are still the heart and soul of the nation's education system in spite of the attacks they have endured. The annual Phi Delta Kappa/Gallup Poll of the Public's Attitudes Toward the Public Schools regularly has shown that, in spite of the concerns that Americans express about the nation's public schools, they have been satisfied with the one their child attends.

Public education has long supported American democracy. Our task is to make sure it continues to do so in our future. I have identified eight considerations that public education needs to address. Undoubtedly there are many other possibilities, but the following will provide us with a good starting point.

1. The Kudzu Phenomenon. In the September 2002 issue of the *Phi Delta Kappan,* John Goodlad talked about the kudzu vine, a plant which is capable of growing one foot a day. It was introduced to the United States in 1876 to shade the porches of southern mansions and reintroduced during the 1940s to combat erosion. While it does help erosion, it grows so fast that it is capable of killing forests; and an estimated $50 million per year is required to combat it. Kudzu is a wonderful metaphor for the education "reforms" that have been foisted on the profession by overzealous politicians who wish to be elected president, governor, or any number of political offices. We are being "kudzued" by politicians who prostitute the public education profession in their campaigns. Usually their political ads mention more testing, more homework, and more time spent on the "three R's." Never do they quote any research that would provide validity for their "reforms." Nor do these politicians argue for the enabling legislation that would provide funding for their reforms.

We need to say NO to these reforms proposed by politicians who have neither the background as educators nor the research to validate their schemes and who fail to enact the enabling legislation.

2. Identify "Blue-Ribbon Backers" of Public Education. This one would be fun.

Throughout our history we've had many brilliant Americans who have championed public education. We should give credit to these past champions of public education. First on the list, of course, is Thomas Jefferson. Others include such presidents as Jimmy Carter, who created the Secretary of Education as a cabinet-level position, and Lyndon Johnson, a public school product who championed the notion of equal education opportunities in so many ways. Such public education stalwarts as Horace Mann, John Dewey, and John Goodlad also need to be constantly studied and revered for all of their positive influences.

3. Use Teachers as Decision Makers. No other profession relies on outsiders to make professional decisions as much as does the education profession. Politicians, corporate CEOs, and other noneducators are involved in making far too many decisions about what goes on in American classrooms. Recently there has been a mini-revolution against HMO executives who trump the decisions of medical doctors. Professional teachers know more about teaching kids and evaluating their education performance than does anyone else. Their knowledge and expertise must supercede the agendas of noneducators.

4. Counterattack High-Stakes Testing. High-stakes testing programs do not tell us what we need to know about the effectiveness of public education. Instead, the data tell us that what we really are measuring is little more than the level of affluence that exists in a single school, school district, or state. In addition, the tests we now use are incapable of measuring higher thinking skills, particularly synthesis and evaluation. These tests are machine scored, and only humans can measure the top levels of cognitive functioning.

There are better ways to measure student performance. First, we can ask teachers. Years ago the Harvard Graduate Study told us that principals and teachers could predict the college success of students more accurately than could test scores or grade point averages. So, if public education is to become the guardian of our democratic society, we need to reestablish the kind of respect for public teachers that existed during the first half of the last century. In this, we should take a lesson from Japan. Japanese teachers, or "sensei," are highly revered. The same reverence for public school teachers must be reestablished in the United States.

5. Improve Teacher Education. It is imperative for teacher education programs to teach students how to implement strand-planning strategies that continuously address multicultural issues. Moreover, preservice teachers must have ample opportunities to work with students from different cultural backgrounds. These experiences must be monitored and directed by persons who are experts in the field of multicultural education. In addition, schools of education need to improve the percentage of minority-group members on their faculties. Currently, only 5% of university faculties are identified as members of minority groups.

6. Follow the First Amendment. The Establishment Clause of the First Amendment is quite clear; it does not allow tax money to pay for private religious education. However, a multitude of efforts are under way by right-leaning groups of all types to institute voucher programs and other ploys to fund private religious schools with public tax money. If these efforts succeed, the support of the public school system in the United States could be seriously compromised. Persons committed to the maintenance of the nation's public schools should fight such efforts with all their energy.

7. Beware of Businesses Bearing Gifts. Many schools and school districts have become involved in alliances with various business interests that claim to be interested in "reforming" public education. "Adopt a school programs" have been popular in many cities. Some of these programs have been successful, but others have not. Some business factions have been interested in privatizing public schools. And, of course, some school districts have employed private companies to operate their schools, particularly in large cities. While there have been a few marginally successful programs, we must never forget the basic nature of American business interests. *They exist to make a profit.* That is not a bad thing, but it has no place in schools.

Schools are not businesses. Business models do not work in schools. Before any public school makes an alliance with a business, the educators must always ask "What am I giving up if I engage in a relationship with this business? What do they want from us? What kinds of concessions will they require for their financial backing?"

8. Establish a Public School Task Force. I have mentioned several prominent backers of public education, from Thomas Jefferson to John Goodlad. There are other highly influential figures from education, politics, and other walks of life who are passionate about the importance of public schools in a democratic society. We need to enlist their services and their support. There is a battle pending for the survival of our public schools. We must enlist all the advocates we can find, and we must be willing to fight.

EDUCATION FOR DEMOCRACY:
Liberal, Conservative, or Does It Matter?

DONOVAN R. WALLING

It is like singing *The Star-Spangled Banner*; the words come easily through long familiarity: "Democracy serves the common good of our nation." In theory, democracy gives all of the people equal voice in running their government. Ergo, a principal role of *public* education is to teach democratic values and processes so that an informed citizenry can wisely exercise its democratic rights and responsibilities. That is the gist of Thomas Jefferson's vision.

Those are good words, but it's getting the tune right that's hard. Orchestrating public schools to teach and model democracy, particularly in the face of today's countervailing forces, is as challenging for states and local communities as it is for most of us to hit the high notes of Francis Scott Key's borrowed melody.

American democracy has sputtered into the 21st century more challenged than at any time in recent memory. American democratic principles took a drubbing after the terrorist attacks of 11

Donovan R. Walling is director of Publications and Research for Phi Delta Kappa International. He formerly taught English and art in the Sheboygan, Wisconsin, public schools and for the Department of Defense Dependents Schools in Germany and was an education administrator in Wisconsin and Indiana. Walling is the author of books, monographs, and articles on numerous education topics.

September 2001. One need look no further than the USA Patriot Act, which was rushed into law only 45 days after 9/11. The act legitimizes expanded government surveillance and investigative powers, in some instances with little or no relation to terrorism, and reduces the checks and balances on the executive branch that are a keystone of democracy.

Patriotic fervor — the act passed 98 to 1 in the Senate and 356 to 66 in the House — cannot be substituted for reason if democracy is to survive, much less to thrive. The ills of overly zealous patriotism are legion. After all, most terrorists are simply overly zealous patriots for their own causes. Such "patriotism" perverts the course of democracy. Fortunately, democracy tends to self-correct over time, though much damage can be done in the meantime.

We often talk as if democracy were one *thing*. In truth, democracy is many things, many interpretations, depending on where it is practiced and by whom. American democracy is a nationalistic concept, one that is idealized for domestic consumption, both inside classrooms and in the larger society. In practice, of course, our brand of democracy (and, to be fair, everyone else's) is far from ideal.

Democracy means "government by the people," from the Greek *demos,* meaning "people." Abraham Lincoln succinctly stated our notion of the concept in the closing sentence of his address on the Gettysburg battlefield: "government of the people, by the people, for the people."

But realistically, our *demos* is, and always has been, variously defined; and it seldom includes everyone. Pure one-citizen/one-vote democracy, though technically feasible in the 21st century, remains unrealized. Everyone got a reminder of this fact with the election of George W. Bush in 2000. He lost the popular vote, the vote truly "by the people." But, with little more than a shrug of nine robed shoulders, he was handed the presidency anyway because, errors and shenanigans aside, he carried the electoral vote.

The Electoral College is an extension of representative democracy. The second President Bush was not the first candidate to win the high office on the electoral vote after losing the popular vote.

In 1888, for example, that was how Benjamin Harrison took the presidency for four years between Grover Cleveland's two terms in the White House. Harrison lost the popular vote by 100,456 votes, a narrower margin than Bush's 540,520 votes. The public "corrected" the situation four years later, putting President Cleveland back in office. I will leave it to historians to debate whether that was a smart move.

In a country of more fervent politics, we might have seen widespread riots at this type of result. But in the United States, our notion of representative, rather than direct, democracy meant that we, too, would shrug our collective shoulders and move on. Or was it the fact that most of us simply didn't care? In 2000 only 51.3% of all eligible voters went to the polls to cast their ballot. Is it still "democracy" when only half of the *demos* takes part?

Self-correction is now at work with regard to the USA Patriot Act. The act is an example of legislation that resonates on a visceral level but fails to hold up when tasked on the details. Thus democratic *reason* may be better found in the voices of a growing number of citizens opposed to the USA Patriot Act. Those voices are rising in volume, as attested by a growing list of state and municipal resolutions denouncing the act as a threat to civil liberties. The act has, in the minds of this growing number, failed a litmus test: It does *not* serve the common good. Instead, it jeopardizes our democracy.

The USA Patriot Act also is an example of "pass now, fix later" legislation, laws rushed through the legislative process for one reason or another that, later on, need to be revised substantially if not discarded altogether. This is by no means a new problem, and it is not limited to the federal legislature. The landmark *Brown* v. *Board of Education*, though not "rushed" per se, was decided by the Supreme Court in 1954 only to be revisited the next year in *Brown (II)*, which said that the desegregation mandated in *Brown* should proceed with "all deliberate speed." The 1954 decision simply said desegregation ought to happen, not how fast.

More recently, the No Child Left Behind Act of 2001 fits the description of "pass now, fix later." Signed by President George

W. Bush on 8 January 2002, NCLB is a law that *sounds* good. Who can argue with the sentiment of leaving no child behind? The primary purpose of this law is to ensure that every child gets the best possible education and to close the achievement gap between poor and affluent children.

Like the USA Patriot Act, NCLB enjoyed broad bipartisan support in Congress. When the bill emerged from the conference committee, it passed the House 381 to 41 and the Senate 87 to 10. But also like the USA Patriot Act, NCLB's flaws soon began to come to light. Many critics now believe that the legislation is profoundly flawed, both conceptually and procedurally. For example, a key issue has been the rush to label schools as "failing" under the law in order to gain assistance for those schools — assistance left largely to states to provide in an era when education funding is particularly tight. (The law is seriously underfunded at the federal level.) Unsurprisingly the schools labeled as "failing" have invariably been those with high concentrations of students from impoverished families or high percentages of special needs students. These are precisely the students who have always needed more assistance, both educational and economic, and have seldom received it. The law is a pointing finger, not a helping hand.

However, this labeling issue is overshadowed by the idealism that is the real flaw of the act. The law's mandate that *every* child in America demonstrate (according to high-stakes testing) proficiency by 2013-14 might "sound good" but is nonsense. NCLB would have schools focus on activities grounded in "statistically based research" but ignores the fact that there is no research to support the idealistic belief that every child *can* learn to a high level, or at least can learn what will be tested to a high level. And to expect *every* child to reach proficiency in *every* school within 12 years is not only wishful thinking but also self-defeating rhetoric. Such impracticality ensures that the law will fail. Thus the pragmatic question becomes, How much damage will NCLB cause in the meantime?

The No Child Left Behind Act espouses a sentiment that resonates with our national sense of the common good. Everyone wants all children to succeed. That we often invest this ideal with more hope than action is beside the point — except that *laws* can not be merely expressions of hope. Laws are intended to result in action. They may not spell out what action should be taken, but they state what result is desired or expected, a goal toward which the implementers of the law must work. If the goal is reasonable, then the law can succeed. If the goal is merely the expression of an ideal, then the law is doomed to failure. But laws being what they are, a good deal of usually expensive wheel-spinning will be done before a failed law can be changed, rescinded, or simply abandoned. Democratic self-correction is by no means quick or cheap.

NCLB requires every student to master English and math. The law's goal is absolute, 100% mastery by all students regardless of any limiting factor. The framers of NCLB did not ignore limiting factors, such as mental and physical handicaps, disparate socio-economic circumstances, and the like. Indeed, imbedded in NCLB is the requirement that such limiting factors be pointed out — and then overcome. For everyone.

Any reasonable person will readily discern that the No Child Left Behind Act is irrational and doomed to failure. So why make such a law? Three possible rationales come to mind, all admittedly somewhat cynical:

- NCLB asserts an egalitarian proposition, namely that in a free society no child should be deprived of an adequate education for any reason. The *Declaration of Independence* asserts that all people are "created equal" in the same sense. These are ideals, likely unreachable, but toward which people must strive for the common good. They are ideals that lie at the heart of our democracy, involving as they do the entire *demos*. In its way, NCLB is profoundly patriotic.
- NCLB is anti-liberal in the modern sense of liberal arts as validating the worth of all knowledge. By identifying English and math as subjects of most worth, the framers of NCLB have asserted that it is not sufficient for any student to be

mildly interested and successful in these subjects but enthusi-
astic about, say, history or art or music or auto mechanics to
the point of excellence. NCLB would shave off the corners
and get all of the pegs into the round holes of English and
math mastery, regardless of talent or interest to the contrary.
Back-to-basics proponents can applaud this rationale.

- NCLB's framers expect schools to fail, as all schools eventually will, given the 100% success expectation. The standard is
perfection in an imperfect world. That the law has been consistently underfunded further ensures failure. Radical conservatives, particularly those on the Religious Right, will be able
to point to the failure of the public schools as further, perhaps
compelling evidence that the public schools should be dis-
mantled and that American education should be privatized.
This is a profoundly anti-democratic view, because the goal
in this case is to reshape our society into something other than
a democracy.

None of these rationales, from the ideal to the anti-democratic,
can be said to serve the common good as most Americans, I sus-
pect, understand it.

The imperative of what in modern terms is called a liberal education is to meet the needs of a diverse population of students.
Political conservatives often paint this form of mass education
with "liberal" as a pejorative. But is not the preservation of our
historical values, of which diversity is demonstrably one, a highly conservative endeavor?

Public education in a democracy, in order to serve the common
good, must teach and model democratic values. Those values at
the core assert the worth of the individual — those who are square
pegs as well as those who are round pegs. Individual worth, col-
lected, *is* the common good of the nation.

Our inherent strength in the United States is our diversity. And
that diversity applies to education, such that every individual
must have the opportunity to learn according to his or her needs,
interests, and talents. "Sound good" laws, such as NCLB and the

USA Patriot Act, work to the detriment of the common good, however well intended they may be, because they tear at the fabric of our freedom and individuality.

Since its dedication in 1886, the Statue of Liberty has stood as a symbol, welcoming immigrants to our shores and reminding us of the virtue and value of a diverse nation, a nation of many talents, many modes of excellence. As a nation, however, we have been challenged by events in this new century. Global terrorism has frightened us, and the direct effect of terrorism felt at home has been to allow our historical freedoms to be curtailed or diminished through such measures as the USA Patriot Act. Since the events of 9/11, the Statue of Liberty has been closed to visitors. Euphemistically, according to the statue website: "Due to improvements and ongoing construction upgrades currently in progress, the Statue of Liberty remains closed until further notice. . . . No date for re-opening has been set" (www.nps.gov/stli, visited 12 February 2004). The USA Patriot Act has in some respects closed more than symbolic doors on Americans' freedoms.

Narrow, unwarranted, unwieldy (and too often underfunded) federal legislation aimed at schools, of which the No Child Left Behind Act is most notable, has a similar chilling effect on education for democracy. Education leaders are justifiably as skeptical of NCLB as civil libertarians are of the USA Patriot Act. Will these acts ultimately do more harm than good?

No Child Left Behind, contrary to its title, eventually will leave most children and their schools behind in the quest for excellence as the law defines it. The constricted priorities set by NCLB do not serve the common good because the "every peg must be round" vision embodied in the law is contrary to our historical strength in diversity — and fundamentally contrary to human nature.

TAKE BACK PUBLIC EDUCATION:
A Task for Intellectuals in a Time of Crisis

HENRY A. GIROUX AND SUSAN SEARLS GIROUX

The current crisis of U.S. public education provides an opportunity to speculate on two aspects of post-civil-rights America. The first has to do with the current state of American political culture: the declining interest in and cynicism about mainstream national politics, its decidedly negative effect on the democratic process, and how such entrenched dispositions might be reversed. The second has to do with the nation's increasing skepticism, even overt hostility, toward the education system at all levels.

When individuals are unable to translate their privately suffered misery into broadly shared public concerns and collective action, democracy is imperiled. Multinational corporations are shaping the content of most media and privatizing the remaining public spaces, which has made civic engagement appear impotent and rendered public values invisible. Political exhaustion and impoverished intellectual visions are fed by the increasingly popular assumption that there are no alternatives to the present state of affairs.[1]

For many people today, citizenship is about the act of buying and selling commodities, rather than increasing the scope of their

Henry A. Giroux holds the Global Television Network Chair in Communications at McMaster University. Susan Searls Giroux is an assistant professor of English at McMaster University.

freedoms and rights in order to expand the operations of a substantive democracy. Politics is uncoupled from democratic
values, and market values are coupled with rising bigotry to
undercut the possibility for providing a language in which vital
social institutions can be defended as a public good. And as social
visions of equity recede from public memory, unfettered, brutal
self-interests combine with retrograde social polices to make
security and safety a top domestic priority. One consequence is
that all levels of government, except for those that are related to
the military and police or serve corporate privileges, are being
hollowed out, their role reduced to dismantling the gains of the
welfare state. Government policies now criminalize social problems and prioritize penal methods over social investments. Increasingly, notions of the public cease to resonate as a site of
democratic possibilities, as a fundamental space for how we reac-
tivate our political sensibilities and conceive of ourselves as critical citizens, engaged public intellectuals, and social agents. The
growing lack of justice in American society rises proportionately
to the lack of political imagination and collective hope.[2]

The second aspect of contemporary U.S. culture — that is, the
nation's increasing skepticism and overt hostility toward the education system — also is related to the abandonment of the public
good for private interests.

Equal opportunity to attend quality education institutions —
both public schools and higher education — was one of the defining principles and most potent victories of the civil rights
movement. Schools and universities became more accessible to
minorities, women, and students with disabilities. But the backlash
was immediate; and discontent with such programs as affirmative
action and busing were quite visible by the mid-1970s among
white working-class and middle-class voters, who were feeling
pinched by recession and ignored by the federal government. Yet
most of these people were careful to avoid the overt racism of
their predecessors, who attacked the rights of minority children to
attend desegregated schools or to have access to postsecondary
education.

Public schooling was increasingly defended as a private, rather than a public, good. And with the shift away from public considerations to private concerns, privatization and choice became the catch phrases dominating education reform for the next few decades. The attack on all things public was accompanied by attempts to empty the public treasury; and public education became one of the first targets of neoliberals, neoconservatives, and religious fundamentalists advocating private interests over social needs and democratic values.

With the publication of *A Nation at Risk*, the Reagan Administration gave the green light to pass spending cuts in education — cuts that have been obligatory for each administration to follow. Reconceived as a "big government monopoly," public schooling was derided as bureaucratic, inefficient, and ineffectual, producing a product (dim-witted students) who were singularly incapable of competing in the global marketplace. In short, schools had committed "an act of unthinking, unilateral educational disarmament," the report accused. A clever strategy to be sure, as it provided a ready scapegoat to legitimate the flight of U.S. manufacturing to markets overseas. The increased joblessness and insecurity could be blamed on schools, instead of on the rapacious greed of corporations eager to circumvent U.S. minimum wage laws, federal taxes, and environmental regulations while also breaking the unions at home. Similarly, higher education was accused of being a hotbed of leftist academics who promoted culture wars that derided Western civilization. Higher education was portrayed as the center of a class and race war in which the dreams of the white working class were under attack because of the ideological residue of professors tainted by the legacy of radical Sixties politics; and, in the post-9/11 era, engaging in such dissent was equated with treason. The division and distrust between "elitist liberals" and a white working class was now complete and utterly secure. Employing a mobile army of metaphors drawn from Cold War rhetoric, the Right succeeded in a propaganda campaign to turn the popular tide against public and higher education.

Though there is nothing new in pointing out these two developments — the popular retreat from politics and the disdain of education — we are struck by the fact that they are rarely dealt with as either mutually reinforcing tendencies or as conditions affecting a free and inclusive democratic society. Democratic politics demands the full participation of an educated populace. It demands a public willing to challenge its elected officials and its laws — and change both when necessary. One can't happen without the other; and now it appears both are in jeopardy.

As we've indicated, neither the decline of democracy nor the crisis of education at all levels have gone unnoticed. But curiously, the progressive advocates and activists clustered around each issue have little regard for the other issue. Astute readers of the national political scene have little interest in (and often are woefully ignorant of) the state of education beyond a heartfelt soundbite or two. And educators seem to have lost the language for linking schooling to democracy, convinced that education is now about job training and competitive market advantage. While both sides hold common concerns and seek deliberative action to redress public opinion, both suffer from the retreat from what were core American values — a concern for notions of publicness, equal access and opportunity, equality and autonomy. If the liberal-left seems particularly impotent and disheveled and ineffectual at this point in history, conservatives appear to be the masters of persuasion and organization. Working for decades at grassroots organizing, they have taken both pedagogy and politics deadly seriously. Conversely, mainstream democrats make no mention of an education agenda that differs significantly from the one adopted by the Bush Administration; indeed, they appear split on the far more general issue of a national platform, the majority wanting to occupy a kinder, gentler republicanism in spite of their newly discovered opposition to the war in Iraq, while a few "radicals" seek to reclaim the liberal traditions of the democratic party. Yet we argue that education — both formal and informal, public and higher — should be their first priority.

Let us provide two specific examples of what we mean. First, consider the following statistics: Soon after the invasion of Iraq, the *New York Times* released a survey indicating that 42% of the American public believed that Saddam Hussein was directly responsible for the September 11 attacks on the World Trade Center and the Pentagon. CBS also released a news poll indicating that 55% of the public believed that Saddam Hussein directly supported the terrorist organization Al Qaeda. A Knight Ridder/Princeton Research poll found that "44% of respondents said they thought 'most' or 'some' of the September 11, 2001, hijackers were Iraqi citizens." A majority of Americans also believed that Saddam Hussein had weapons of mass destruction, that such weapons had been found, that he was about to build a nuclear bomb, and that he eventually would unleash it on an unsuspecting American public. None of these claims had any basis in fact, as no evidence existed to even remotely confirm these assertions. What does this represent, if not a crisis of pedagogy — both formally and informally — in the public sphere?

Of course, these opinions were legitimated by President Bush, Vice President Cheney, Colin Powell, and Condolezza Rice and reproduced uncritically by the media. These misrepresentations and strategic distortions circulated in the popular press either with uncritical, jingoistic enthusiasm, as in the case of the Fox News Channel, or through the dominant media's refusal to challenge such claims — both positions, of course, in opposition to such foreign news sources as the BBC, which repeatedly challenged these assertions. Such deceptions are never innocent, and in this case they appear to have been used shamelessly by the Bush Administration to muster support for both the Iraq invasion and an ideological agenda "that overwhelmingly favors the president's wealthy supporters and is driving the federal government toward a long-term fiscal catastrophe."[3]

The Bush Administration's war against Iraq should be seen in the context of the war being waged at home against the young. As Senator Robert Byrd stated in a Senate floor speech, President Bush has no trouble asking Congress for $87 billion in supplemental funds to rebuild Iraq but refuses to allocate the $6 billion needed to fund his education reform program or, for that matter, the resources needed to support education programs for our neediest students. As Byrd puts it, "I wonder how the Senators who object to the cost of my amendment . . . to add $6.1 billion for Title I education programs to fully fund money Congress authorized for fiscal year 2004 . . . will view the President's request to add $60 billion or $65 billion or $70 billion to the deficit to fund military and reconstruction activities in Iraq. I wonder if they will be comfortable voting to support a massive spending program for Iraq if they cannot bring themselves to support a comparatively meager increase in education funding for American schoolchildren."[4]

Of course, it will be not only school children who will be suffering from budget shortfalls, but also university students who have to grapple with skyrocketing tuition, decreasing student aid, fewer course offerings delaying graduation, and a generally watered-down education.

Our second example is even more tragic, as we attempt to grapple with the meaning and significance of the torture of Iraqi detainees in Saddam Hussein's most infamous prison, Abu Ghraib. The Bush Administration has been quick to denounce the sadistic behavior of a few rogue individuals for denigrating our alleged claim to moral superiority, or what the President called, "the true nature and heart of America." But recent revelations about the Administration's position that the Geneva Convention's protocol against the torture of prisoners does not protect "unlawful combatants," more incidents of human rights violations in other prisons in Iraq and Afghanistan, and Seymour Hersch's recent claim in the *New Yorker* that Defense Secretary Donald Rumsfeld personally approved interrogation practices legitimating physical assault and mental humiliation suggest that the events at Abu Ghraib were less about what Bush referred to as "failures of character" than about systemic adherence to policies approved at the highest levels of his administration. Perhaps it was an implicit response to the arguments about "chain of command" and "following orders" that emerged from defendants in the weeks that followed the infamous "Sixty Minutes II" report — so eerily reminiscent of Nuremberg — that prompted Susan Sontag to draw careful distinctions between the photographic images of atrocities committed by German soldiers during World War II and pictures of Abu Ghraib. As Sontag notes, in the first instance, executioners almost never placed themselves in the photographs with their victims; but in the second instance, the American soldiers are not only present, but gleeful. "Looking at photographs," she says, "you ask yourself, How can someone grin at the suffering and humiliation of another human being?"[5] It is a ponderous question, one to which we can respond only with more questions.

If we are correct to draw a connection between the failures of a radically underfunded and, for many, decrepit public education system and a profit-driven, corporate-funded mega-media system on the one hand, and a misinformed, politically illiterate public on the other, it also is possible to point to another form of illiteracy — a moral and ethical illiteracy — as a direct consequence of such grossly inadequate institutions once entrusted to enable democracy. What happens in the absence of critical thought, when blind obedience hardens into boredom, reflection gives way to narcissism, passivity finds solace in extreme and often violent spectacles, and humiliation and despair give way to obscene debauchery? Finding no decent answer to such failures of the nation's schools, there is, it seems, a military answer, as Jonothan Kozol once argued, an "all-American and patriotic answer: basic training, absolute obedience to flag and anthem, suspension of emotion in the face of death, a certain hedonistic joy . . . at the prospect of mechanical annihilation."[6] For those who respond to the crisis of the nation's schools with a demand for work skills, for those who see zero tolerance as the answer to any teen infraction, for those who insist that the nation's professoriate "aim low" in their efforts to shape character and fashion citizens, we ask, after Kozol, "Is this the kind of literacy we want? Is this the best that Jeffersonian democracy can do?"[7]

One of the central tenets of modern democracy is that a democracy cannot exist without educated citizens. However, the media have extended, if not superceded, institutionalized education as the most important educational force in developed societies. This does not invalidate the enormous importance of formal education to democracy, but it does require a recognition of how the work of education takes place within other spheres, or sites, of pedagogy, such as news, advertising, television, film, the Internet, videogames, and the popular press. It also underscores the significance of formal spheres of learning that — unlike their popular counterparts, which are driven largely by commercial interests that more often mis-educate the public — must provide citizens with those critical capacities, modes of literacies, knowledge, and skills that enable them to both read the world and participate in shaping and governing it. It is not that public education is a disinterested space, but that in its best moments it works through altogether different interests than the commercial values promoted by corporations. That is, public education self-consciously educates future citizens capable of participating in and reproducing a democratic society. In spite of their present embattled status and contradictory roles, universities and colleges remain uniquely placed to prepare students to both understand and influence the larger forces that shape their lives. Such institutions, by virtue of their privileged position and dedication to freedom and democracy, have an obligation to draw on those traditions and resources capable of providing a liberal and humanistic education to all students in order to prepare them for a world in which information and power have taken on new and powerful dimensions.[8]

Recognizing the inextricable link between education and politics is central to reclaiming public education as a democratic public sphere. So, too, is the recognition that politics cannot be separated from pedagogy and the sphere of culture. However, acknowledging that pedagogy is political does not mean that it is by default propagandistic, closed, dogmatic, or uncritical of its own authority. Instead, any viable notion of critical pedagogy must demonstrate there is a difference between critical pedagogical practices and propagandizing, critical teaching and demagoguery. Such a pedagogy should be open and discerning, fused with a spirit of inquiry that fosters, rather than mandates, critical modes of individual and social agency. Pedagogy should provide the theoretical tools and resources necessary for understanding how culture works as an educational force, how public education connects to other sites of pedagogy, and how identity, citizenship, and agency are organized through pedagogical relations and practices. Rather than viewing pedagogy as a technical method, it must be understood as a moral and political practice that always presupposes particular renditions of what constitutes legitimate knowledge, values, citizenship, modes of understanding, and views of the future. Thus pedagogy should provide the classroom conditions that provide the knowledge, skills, and culture of questioning necessary for students to engage in critical dialogue with the past, question authority and its effects, struggle with ongoing relations of power, and prepare themselves for what it means to be critically active citizens in the interrelated local, national, and global public spheres.

If public education is a crucial sphere for creating citizens who are equipped to exercise their freedoms and competent to question the basic assumptions that govern democratic political life, then academics will have to assume their responsibility as citizen-scholars by taking critical positions, relating their work to larger social issues, offering students knowledge and dialogue about pressing social problems, and providing the conditions for students not only to have hope and the belief that civic life matters, but that they can make a difference in shaping it so as to expand its democratic possibilities for all groups.

Educators now face the daunting challenge of creating new discourses, pedagogical practices, and collective strategies that will offer students and others the hope and tools necessary to revive the culture of politics as an ethical response to the demise of democratic public life. Such a challenge suggests struggling to keep alive those institutional spaces that support critical education, that help students come to terms with their own power as individual and social actors, and that provide the conditions for students to learn how to take risks and exercise civic courage and compassion. Educators must engage in teaching and research that is socially responsible while refusing to surrender our knowledge and skills to the highest bidder.

Another important challenge facing educators is the need to address the ongoing role that racial politics has played in shaping the curriculum, as well as more general questions of how race structures access to and opportunity within public education. One approach might center on addressing the series of intellectual shifts from classical rhetoric to philology to an aesthetic formalism that redefines culture as nonpolitical, universal, and race-free. Such an analysis can illustrate that the contemporary call for a "return" to a thoroughly deracinated, formal engagement with the disciplines that make up the curriculum is impossible because race has always been a part of that construction. Interconnecting philosophical, political, and social forces affect school curricula. Specifically, Social Darwinism and racial science, as well as mass European immigration, posed significant challenges to the classical liberal principles that shaped an active and critical citizenry.

Equally important is the need to address the rolling back of opportunity and access for minority students at all levels of schooling, which is being accomplished by iniquitous tax-funding schemes, debates over "standards," and overt attacks on "politically correct" curricula, programs, and funding programs for minority students. This post-civil rights backlash not only threatens the civic mission of public schools to prepare all citizens for participation in self-government, but also undermine any pretense to "freedom" and "equality" — tenets once central to liberal democratic politics.

Another challenge that needs to be addressed is the threat that neoliberalism and corporate values pose to public education. We need to remind ourselves that democratic, rather than commercial, values should be the primary concerns of schools and universities. While public education should equip students to enter the workplace, it should also educate them to contest workplace inequalities, to imagine democratically organized forms of work, and to identify and challenge those injustices that contradict and undercut the most fundamental principles of freedom, equality, and respect for all people.

But public education is about more than job preparation and raising critical consciousness. It also is about imagining different futures. In contrast to the cynicism and political withdrawal that the media foster, a critical education demands that its citizens be able to translate the interface of private considerations and public issues; to be able to recognize those undemocratic forces that deny social, economic, and political justice; and to be willing to give some thought to their experiences as a matter of anticipating and struggling for a better world.

If right-wing reforms in public education continue unchallenged, the consequence will be a bifurcated civic body. In other words, we will have a society in which a highly trained, largely white elite will be allowed to command the techno-information revolution while a low-skilled majority of poor and minority workers will be relegated to filling the McJobs proliferating in the service sector. Neither will be equipped to make ethical judgments about the world around them. Education must not be confused with training; and if educators and others are to prevent this distinction from becoming blurred, it is crucial for them to challenge the ongoing corporatization of public schools while upholding the legacy of a social contract in which all youth can hope for a democratic future. We need to embrace Protestant theologian Deitrich Bonhoeffer's belief that the ultimate test of morality for any democratic society resides in the condition of its children.

To "take back public education" is not a call for any one political ideology to take over the public schools. Instead, it means to take a stand on public education's crucial role in educating students to participate in an inclusive democracy. It is a call to action for educators, parents, students, and others to reclaim public education as a democratic public sphere, a place where teaching is not confused with training and propaganda, a safe space where reason, understanding, dialogue, and critical engagement are available to all faculty and students. Public education must become a site of ongoing struggle to preserve and extend the conditions in which autonomy of judgment and freedom of action are informed by the democratic imperatives of equality, liberty, and justice. It is education that makes possible our students' democratic identities, values, and politics.

Notes

1. See Jeffrey C. Goldfarb, *The Cynical Society: The Culture of Politics and the Politics of Culture in American Life* (Chicago: University of Chicago Press, 1991); Joseph N. Capella and Kathleen Hall Jamieson, *Spiral of Cynicism: The Press and the Public Good* (New York: Oxford University Press, 1997); Russell Jacoby, *The End of Utopia* (New York: Basic Books, 1999); William Chaloupka, *Everybody Knows: Cynicism in America* (Minneapolis: University of Minnesota Press, 1999); Zygmunt Bauman, *In Search of Politics* (Stanford, Calif.: Stanford University Press, 1999); Carl Boggs, *The End of Politics: Corporate Power and the Decline of the Public Sphere* (New York: Guilford, 2000); Henry A. Giroux, *Public Spaces, Private Lives: Democracy Beyond 9-11* (Boulder, Colo.: Rowman and Littlefield, 2003); Theda Skocpol, *Diminished Democracy* (Norman: University of Oklahoma Press, 2003).
2. See Roberto Mangabeira Unger and Cornel West, *The Future of American Progressivism* (Boston: Beacon Press, 1998).
3. Bob Herbert, "The Art of False Impression," *New York Times*, 11 August 2003, p. A17.
4. Sen. Robert Byrd, "From Bad to Worse . . . Billions for War on Iraq, A Fraction for Poor Kids' Education," Senate floor remarks, 5 September 2003.
5. Susan Sontag, "Regarding the Torture of Others: Notes on What Has Been Done — and Why — to Prisoners by Americans," *New York Times Sunday Magazine*, 23 May 2004, p. 28.
6. Jonothan Kozol, *Illiterate America* (New York: Anchor Press, Doubleday, 1985), p. 85.
7. Ibid., p. 86.
8. This issue is discussed by Stanley Aronowitz, *The Knowledge Factory* (Boston: Beacon Press, 2000).

DEMOCRACY, EDUCATION, AND A FREE PRESS:
Beyond the Cliché

DENIS P. DOYLE

Education not only makes democracy possible; it also makes it essential. Education not only brings into existence a population with an understanding of the public tasks; it also creates their demand to be heard.
— J.K. Galbraith, *Good Society*

And ye shall know the truth, and the truth shall make you free. — John 8:32
— Inscribed on the wall of the main lobby, Central Intelligence Agency Headquarters

If a nation expects to be ignorant and free, in a state of civilization, it expects what never was and never will be.
— Thomas Jefferson

In America at least, the ideas of democracy, education, and a free press are so closely bound together that it is difficult to separate the hard kernels of truth from the easy platitudes. The easy platitudes, of course, are the stuff of commencement addresses: *Know the truth and the truth will make you free.* Or Jefferson and

Denis P. Doyle is co-founder and chief academic officer of SchoolNet, a Web-enabled school reform company, and editor of *The Doyle Report,* an e-news letter on technology and education. He is the author of numerous books and articles about education reform, which can be found at www.thedoyle report.com. He can be reached at denis@schoolnet.com.

the other Founders had it right: *For democracy to function the people must be educated.* Or a free press is essential to democracy. All true, of course, but so casually accepted and so widely praised that the underlying truth is attenuated. Which is to say, the ideas bear re-examination. Or more forcefully, perhaps, the defense of democracy, education, and a free press falls to each generation anew.

The hard kernel of truth, of course, is that we are a young country but an old democracy. We fought a revolution to establish a democratic republic, and it has endured. Its twin pillars are mass education and a free press. But historical memory is short.

As an educated citizenry is essential to effective democracy, so too is a free press. Education gives us the ground to stand on, a free press the opportunity to use our education, and democracy the forum in which it is expressed.

While democracy and education today look much as they always have, technology has transformed the concept of a free press. Much more than hard copy — newspapers and magazines, broadsides and pamphlets — today's publication opportunities are most broadly thought of in terms of IT (information technology). IT includes a bewildering array of communication tools, from traditional newspapers, magazines, and journals to online news; from national TV networks to low wattage FM radio; from PDAs (personal digital assistants) with e-mail and Web capabilities to cable TV; from anytime-anywhere access to the World Wide Web to low-cost on-demand publishing. The list is long and growing, prices are falling, and capacities increasing.

For example, the Federal Communications Commission has approved (in February 2004) inexpensive Web access over household electricity lines; with a $30 modem it will be possible to get Internet access from any outlet in the house (from those utilities that support the service). The World Wide Web, of course, is a genuine revolution; and for a peek into the future we need only look at Japan, where nearly half the population uses cell phones with e-mail and Web access.

Indeed, it was pamphleteering — Thomas Paine's *Common Sense* — that started the American Revolution. IT is simply its modern extension. But it is more than that; IT is a transforming technology, going beyond the traditional reach of a conventional free press. Hard copy requires consequential capital investment; and in the days of hand-set type and letter presses, it was labor as well as capital intensive. By contrast, websites and Web access are available to anyone who can scrape together a few dollars. And if traditional print journalism was elitist, IT is radically democratic. In some respects, the effect has been less noticeable in America because our traditions of a free press are so old and so deep that we take them for granted. Not so in other parts of the world.

IT as "free press" first surfaced as a global phenomenon with Tiananmen Square, with the so-called fax revolution (by which device students and intellectuals evaded the censors to communicate among themselves and to get their message out; their dismay at losing was all the more poignant for that). But it had its origins several decades ago with the *Samizdat* behind the iron curtain, self-publishing intellectuals and dissidents who escaped the censors and reached small but important audiences because of the advent of the compact PC and small personal printer. (Until that time they had been limited to portable typewriters and carbon paper, a source of unparalleled frustration some of us still remember only too well from college and graduate school.)

Then there is a powerful modern example close to home in Democratic Governor and would-be presidential nominee Howard Dean. His extraordinary use of the Web is the latest chapter in this unfolding drama. His campaign transformed the American political scene. (That his campaign later imploded makes the fundamental revolution he unleashed all the more interesting.) In a matter of months, using the Web, he raised $40 million in small contributions, an unprecedented event. At the same time, he used the Web as a grassroots organizing and communications tool. Although it may look like so much nerd heaven, it is a development that will resonate for years to come. Indeed, its contours and effect are only beginning to be understood.

IT Central to Modern Democracy

It is clear then, that the three ideas — democracy, education, and a free press — are inextricably interlocked. Most important, I would argue, is IT, for it is both emblematic and the actual representation of all three. Not only is IT central to modern democratic processes, from fundraising and informing voters to actually voting (with touch screens, for example), it is central to education, both as a means of content delivery and a means of expression.

The interaction effects of democracy, education, and IT are sharply revealed in the Second and Third Worlds. China, for example, has an increasingly well-educated middle class with growing access to the Web. Can democracy be far behind? Can the great Chinese economic engine, now revving up, be sustained without a massive investment in education? Can an educated citizenry be denied self-expression and self-rule?

The underlying question, of course, is how are democratic traditions secured? Can they be imported the way goods and service are, or must they grow organically as they did in the OECD countries? (The Organization of Economic Cooperation and Development is composed of the countries with advanced — "postindustrial," as Peter Drucker would say — economies. All are democracies, though in the case of several members, notably Japan and Germany, democracy was a mid-20th century import.)

In the same vein, how should people be educated, and what role does IT have to play? For my part, the answers interlock and reinforce each other. As a people, across the globe:

- We must be educated in the liberal arts.
- We must be educated by three instrumentalities: study, example, and practice, which is not only sound pedagogy but reinforces democratic habits of mind.
- We must understand that IT is a transforming and liberating technology and deploy it as such.

Liberal Education

Why must we be liberally educated? Simply this: Only a liberal education prepares us for the vicissitudes and uncertainties of modern life, for the moral challenges and tough choices that we face over time and day to day. To be sure, science and technology are the defining elements of the 20th and 21st centuries. All the more reason to infuse them with the broad and deep knowledge that a liberal education seeks to impart. Imagine the world of the late 19th century, without electricity, air travel, TV, and computers. Or imagine a world without antibiotics or modern medicine. Thanks to science and technology, both are a vanishing memory. But the fact remains that the wise use of science and technology is the province of ethics and morality, the liberal arts. Science and technology uninformed by a moral vision are amoral at best, Dr. Frankenstein's monster at worst. At the extreme, science and technology, uniformed by the moral sense, lead to the death camps of the totalitarian state.

But first things first. By democracy, of course, we mean rule of the people, or self-rule, from the Greek *demos*. Education means many things, most commonly and wrongly, training. (Animals are trained, people educated is the old adage.) There is, however, a more nuanced and elevated meaning from its Latin derivation, *educare,* to draw out. Or as Webster's *Collegiate Encyclopedia* defines it: *the transmission of the values and accumulated knowledge of a society*. That is education at its best. Democracy, to succeed, requires a particular kind of education, *education for life in the polis*, to which I return shortly.

How deceptively close the terms *democracy* and *education* seem. But it was not always so. Self-rule, once thought to mean direct democracy, can also be interpreted to mean limited democracy, as it was in ancient Greece and Rome, or representative democracy, as it is widely practiced today. Indeed, it was from the traditions of limited democracy that the concept of a liberal education arose. A liberal education is no more and no less than the education suited for a free person, as distinct from a slave. *Liberalis*. Free. And its purpose is not vocational or practical. To the contrary, its purpose is to suit men and women to lead lives of ordered liberty. And as we would all be free, we must, perforce, be liberally educated.

By liberal education the ancients meant the arts of rhetoric and persuasion, of reasoned discourse, rational thought, and conversation. To be sure, discourse could degenerate into sophistry — the words of a *wise fool*, extant to this day in the concept of the sophomore — but that was a failing, not a virtue. True virtue, civic virtue, was realized through the development of a moral compass that was not inborn but acquired.

Perhaps most important, a liberal education stands in precise contradistinction to orthodoxy of any and all kinds, religious, ideological, or scientific. A liberal education develops habits of mind that are essential to both democracy and science (and are hostile to ideology): toleration of differences, an abiding interest in free and unfettered inquiry, a respect for self and others, a willingness to re-examine premises and findings, and an ability to face life with confidence in the face of uncertainty and ambiguity. Of one thing a liberal education is sure: There are no non-negotiable certainties. No set of values could be further removed from orthodoxy, particularly theocracy, whether of the medieval Christian Church, Orthodox Judaism, or the theocracy of much of modern Islam. Indeed, functioning democracy enshrines a respect for differences that is the polar opposite of orthodoxy.

And how is it acquired? Study, example, and practice are ideas that go back to the ancient Greeks — to Aristotle, for example, for whom one acquires virtue by behaving virtuously. One studies virtue, one practices it, one is an example of the virtuous life. "What is happiness?" Aristotle asks; activity of the soul in accord with perfect virtue, he answers. And on the subject of education, Aristotle has the last word. Asked how much educated men were superior to the uneducated, according to Diogenes Laertius, he said, "As much as the living are to the dead."

Study, Example, Practice

By study, example, and practice the Greeks meant *right* study, *right* example, and *right* practice. Right study is the right curriculum: the facts, ideas, theories, precepts that are foundational knowledge and skills that, once mastered, prepare people to reason and think independently, to draw inferences, and to reach sound conclusions. It includes but is not limited to the great documents of citizenship: the *Magna Carta,* the *Declaration of Independence,* the *Constitution* and *Bill of Rights,* the *Gettysburg Address,* Martin Luther King's *Letter from Birmingham Jail.* And it means much more than rote exposure and memorization. It includes understanding, gained through careful reading, thoughtful discussion, and vigorous debate. All educated Americans should understand, for example, the meaning of the Fifth Amendment; the right not to incriminate oneself is among the most hard won. By prohibiting the state from extracting confessions, the Fifth eliminates the rack and thumbscrew. It eliminates state-sponsored torture.

Right example is the fruit of the examined life, largely a matter of modeling the behavior of the significant adults with whom a student comes in contact. It includes the teacher who loves her discipline, who practices what she preaches. It includes the coach who practices fair play as he imparts skills and knowledge. It includes the music teacher who demonstrates the consequences of practice and study by playing with joy as well as accomplishment. Indeed, right example can be thought of as the invisible curriculum, those attitudes and dispositions that, as Quakers say, are "caught not taught."

There is another dimension to example that bears remembering, and that is the example offered by both historical and fictional figures. Historical figures of note inspire us and help to shape our personas, but so too do fictional figures, from the Robin Hood stories, or the tales of the Brothers Grimm, or *Lord of the Ring.* They do so by striking atavistic chords in us, reminding us that the virtues of honor, courage, and perseverance are not empty platitudes. Indeed, fiction at its best is a way of revealing ultimate truths.

In its simplest form, right practice is learning by doing. It includes practice in its old-fashioned sense, as in practicing the piano. But its more nuanced sense is equally important, as in professional practice, for example, the practice of law or medicine, dance or drama. It means to engage fully with learning as an end in itself, as a process of becoming, as a continual work in progress. Former Charlotte-Mecklenburg Superintendent John Murphy used to be fond of saying that school is not a dress rehearsal.

Taken together over time, study, example, and practice produce the habits of mind of the educated person: a solid knowledge base, continuous curiosity, increasing flexibility, tolerance of others, and willingness to change one's mind when confronted with new evidence. In addition to being the habits of mind of the liberally educated person, they are the habits of the mind of the small *d* democrat. They are what Spanish philosopher George Santayana called "furniture of the mind."

Inevitable Democracy

Democracy cannot flourish unless the citizenry is educated, but there is an important corollary: An educated citizenry can tolerate no other political circumstance but democracy. How better to put one's education to work than self-governance? This has profound significance in the emerging high-tech, global economy. Can China, for example, continue to flourish as an aging oligarchy, or is democracy essential to its long-term success? Indeed, is democracy inevitable as China becomes more and more fully educated? Put most dramatically, can a totalitarian state survive the Web?

Democracy and liberal arts can be measured by their antithesis as well. Their two most irrevocable foes are absolutism and orthodoxy. Indeed, as democracy and liberal education begin to merge, so too do absolutism and orthodoxy. On the one hand, absolutism has a political gloss just as orthodoxy has a religious gloss; but structurally and ideologically the lines between the two are faint. Stalin's communism, Hitler's fascism, Mao's communism have about them nothing so much as religious fervor. And in the present day, religious orthodoxy leads to political theocracy, whether Christian, Jewish, or Muslim.

The habits of mind central to both democracy and liberal education are absolutely foreign to the orthodox and the absolutist; indeed, they are both a reproach to and a threat to absolutism. In biblical interpretation the term is *inerrancy*, meaning that there is but one way to interpret the text. Democracy brooks no such claim. Does this mean that democracy and its companion, liberal education, are hopelessly relativistic, with no intellectual anchor except the fad of the moment? Political theorists since time began have worried about this propensity: rule of the mob is its extreme manifestation. As we are unhappily reminded by recent developments in Haiti, it is dangerous in the extreme and the most serious ill to which democracy can be exposed. The herd mentality. Rush to judgment. Making decisions on the basis of passion rather than reason. In political theory as well as political practice, democracy tends to disorder, autocracy tends to order. Indeed, order was the rallying cry of the Fascist movements of the 1930s in Europe.

It is because of these dangers, real and imagined, that constitution-framers include structural barriers and impediments deliberately to slow the pace of change. Separation of powers and bicameralism are two well-known devices to accomplish this objective, with the more deliberative upper house putting breaks on the more passionate lower house. As the old saw has it, the executive proposes, Congress disposes. And the judiciary interprets. Indeed, it often seems that barriers to action are more numerous and difficult to overturn than opportunities to act.

Democracy in Action

If English character is formed on the playing fields of Eton, American character is formed in the classrooms and assembly halls and on the playing fields of public and private schools across the country. Study, example, and practice, the triptych that defines a learning environment at its best is not limited to academic success. It also is the way that American students absorb democracy. So widespread is the practice that we are apt to take it for granted. Yet in some respects it is uniquely American. On a daily basis American students experience democracy in action, in homerooms, in elections for class officers, in the election of schoolwide officers, in selecting players for teams, in running student clubs and activities. Voting and elections are only a part of the American experience of democracy in action. Democracy also is evident in habits of an easy-going egalitarianism. No one is better than anyone else in America. Anyone can be president. Trial by a jury of peers. Deeply imbued in the American psyche, these attitudes are part and parcel of the American experience.

Indeed, the greatest contribution of democracy properly conceived is the rule of law. It is a pearl beyond price. Its dramatic power is revealed in one of the most enduring novels of the 20th century, *To Kill a Mockingbird*. Who will ever forget Atticus Finch, who, though he lost the case, commanded the moral high ground? Could Scout and Jem have had a better example? Could Cal? Could we?

There is a final and critically important aspect of study, example, and practice that characterizes American schools, and that is the extracurricular environment in which students and staff are steeped. It is so important that it bears re-emphasizing — it is robustly democratic and egalitarian, law-abiding, and embellished with a mini-free press. Student councils, class officers, team captains, club presidents, student courts, student newspapers, and closed-circuit TV are so widespread that they are taken for granted; but they are democracy in action. As well, they are an American invention, not unknown but uncommon abroad, even among the great democracies.

Freedom of the Press in Modern Garb

The hallmark of IT is transparency, which is the hallmark of democracy as well. Which is a segue into the larger question of interaction effects: How do democracy, education, and IT interact? As I have tried to suggest, democracy and education are reciprocals: neither can exist without the other. If popular elections are held among an uneducated populace, there is no way to avoid the rule of the mob. Without education — character formation and a sense of civic duty — there is no restraint on immediate self-interest and majority rule can mean the tyranny of the majority. In a multiparty state it can even mean the tyranny of the plurality. It is sobering to remember that Hitler rose to power through democratic processes. That this permitted him to be a usurper is all the more alarming.

To be sure, constitutional and structural barriers can be erected — as they have been in most democracies — but the surest way to avoid tyranny is to have an educated and well-informed citizenry. As education and democracy are reciprocals, so too is a free press, thereby creating an intellectual and political triangle, the strongest form in nature as well as society. As a free press is central to democracy, it also is central to education. To limit access to information and expression is as hostile to education as it is to democracy.

Conclusion

Jefferson famously said that "if it were left for me to decide whether we should have a government without newspapers, or newspapers without a government, I should not hesitate a moment to prefer the latter." George Will might point out that, strictly speaking, this is the fallacy of the false alternative. Nonetheless, it makes a powerful point. What is at issue is free expression, the free interplay of ideas, the very purpose of education and democracy. Indeed, the quote in its entirety makes that point:

> The basis of our governments being the opinion of the people, the very first object should be to keep that right; and were it left to me to decide whether we should have a government without newspapers, or newspapers without a government, I should not hesitate a moment to prefer the latter. But I should mean that every man should receive those papers and be capable of reading them.

As I opened this essay, so will I close it. The burden of defending freedom falls anew to each generation. The failure to do so leads to freedom's forfeiture. In this connection, I noted in the beginning that democracy and education are relatively unchanged, but that freedom of the press — conceived in terms of IT in particular — has undergone a genuine transformation. This only slightly overstates the case.

Democracy is more expensive than ever thanks to IT. Television advertising is much more costly than print advertising and, because of its format, encourages the debate to sink to a lowest common denominator or worse. But this is what political scientists call an *enabling* not a *causal* circumstance. TV makes anti-intellectualism possible on a huge scale but does not cause it. Education — or its lack — does.

Schools are changing, slowly but surely, and our best public and private schools are very good indeed. That many lag behind may disappoint but is hardly surprising; what is surprising and welcome is the widespread agreement that low performance is unacceptable. True, it will take time to finish the reform work that has begun; but as Mae West said in a slightly different context, anything worth doing well is worth doing slowly.

IT is the wild card, with an unforeseen and unforeseeable capacity to make mischief as well as to do good. There are, for example, websites that assert that the United States never landed on the moon. There are websites about alien abductions. There are websites, no doubt, that assert that the Earth is flat. All the more reason to support education, for the only way to combat ignorance is education. On the upside, there are websites that bring the whole world to us, resources that could only be dimly imagined a decade or two ago. Think of the intellectual wealth of museums alone. Without moving from your laptop, in a matter of minutes (or hours, if the spirit moves you) you can visit the Prado, the National Gallery (in London or Washington, D.C.), the Louvre, and the Chicago Art Institute. And that would be merely a warm-up. The content resources now available are astounding, and they are growing every day.

However, one more source of intellectual power bears mentioning in this context. While it may at first glance may seem banal, it is a pearl beyond price. That is access to public domain information — data and documents — that can be instantaneously retrieved on the Web. The variety and quantity of information is growing explosively. For example, public transactions, both commercial and personal, are now widely available on the Web, ranging from sale prices and tax burdens on real property to Brittany Spears' marriage license (which was on the Clark County website within hours of the nuptials).

In the world of education, IT is transforming both access to and the utility of school information, ranging from online report cards (for students, schools, and districts) to fine-grained data about student and school performance that provide unparalleled analytic and diagnostic opportunities. Indeed, what better collocation of democracy, education, and a free press could be imagined than the opportunity to improve education?

Just as democracy requires transparency to flourish, so does the education process. Historically it was the role of a free press to keep both education and democracy honest. That is what transparency is all about. And that is IT's promise: transparency without precedent.

TOO MUCH DEMOCRACY?

ROBERT P. ENGVALL

Public schools are both a support for democracy and a tool for social control. As an institution, public schools mirror the contradictions in our society; so it is not surprising that they contain both the good and the bad aspects of democracy.

Schooling as a means of controlling the citizenry has a long history in the United States. As Bowles and Gintis point out, "Since its inception in the United States, the public school system has been seen as a method of disciplining children in the interest of producing a properly subordinate adult population . . . the theme of social control pervades educational thought and policy" (2002, p. 93).

The "place" of public schooling in American democracy allows for a divergent series of viewpoints among various groups. Michael Apple describes this divergence in the perceptions of schooling:

> For some groups of people, schooling is seen as a vast
> engine of democracy: opening horizons, ensuring mobility,

Robert P. Engvall is an associate professor of justice studies at Roger Williams University in Rhode Island. Engvall holds J.D. and Ph.D. degrees from the University of Iowa, and he is the author of three books and several articles concerning issues relevant to education in a democracy.

and so on. For others, the reality of schooling is strikingly different. It is seen as a form of social control, or, perhaps, as the embodiment of cultural dangers, institutions whose curricula and teaching practices threaten the moral universe of the students who attend them." (2000, p. 43)

These contradictions are inherent not just in schooling, but in our democracy as well. For example, we speak of one person, one vote, and the inherent "goodness" present in government by and through the people, while at the same time, we allow for ever greater power to be concentrated in the hands of interest groups, corporate America, and a select few. The contradictions are so great that we need to ask whether it is possible to have a strong democracy and such tremendous inequality of wealth and power and whether we can maintain the common good while we become ever more focused on pursuing our individual interests. The answers to these questions are centered on how we educate our citizens.

We first need to determine what is the foremost responsibility of our schools. Is it teaching the "three Rs" or teaching "character"? Perhaps the schools' purpose is to prepare our graduates for the workplace? Where does "citizenship" come into play? How do schools work on behalf of the "common good"?

Democracy demands that citizens be enabled to ask questions of their government. Democracy clearly needs robust debates about the issues, and it needs popular participation in those debates. In turn, education enables us to ask questions in the search for our own truths. Thus education plays a strong role in a democracy.

Not everyone possesses the same oratorical gifts nor the same abilities to reason and debate complicated social and economic issues. Nonetheless, schools must play a vital role in cultivating these abilities among the citizens. Allowing rank or stature to control the debate, while silencing other voices, is antithetical to genuine democracy, despite the fact that such silencing has long been a part of our democracy. Perhaps in our search for "genuine democracy" we must not lose sight of the many flaws within our "practiced democracy."

Apple insists that much of the conservative rhetoric centering on the "decline in the public schools" actually represents a fear of "too much democracy" (2000, p. 91). He suggests that the increased emphasis on "standards" and "testing" really is a method of returning to a meritocracy and away from a genuine democracy. If other government policies favor widening the gaps between the haves and the have-nots, then perhaps government policies toward public schools merely reflect such preferences. If that is true, then our hopes for increased democracy rest on those inside of education.

First we need to examine whether our initial premises about our democracy are, indeed, true. Is our American democracy in good health? Are citizens participating meaningfully in decisions that affect their lives? Do citizens, or even a majority of them, participate at all in these decisions? Edelsky provides a cynical answer to these questions:

> we don't have a democracy. Some of us think we do. Lots of us wish we did. We've got some of the rhetoric and even some of the governmental structures. But we're a long way from living in a democracy. . . .
>
> In a system where wealth buys the right to overrule majority wishes, where wealth buys the power to make decisions that affect the life and livelihood of everybody else, you can't have a democracy. In a system where corporations are so privileged that they can write the laws as well as decide which laws they'll obey, you can't have a democracy. A few can unduly influence decisions in which, if it were a democracy, everybody is supposed to have an equal say. (1999, pp. 147-48)

There is quantitative support for Edelsky's view. For example, the downward trend in voter turnout suggests that fewer voters are willing to take the relatively easy step of even voting in an election. This suggests that more citizens feel powerless and uninvolved with their civic structures. Fewer Americans trust their elected officials to do the right thing; and more Americans believe that special interests, rather than the citizens, control the government.

> Rising voter apathy signals that the issues that matter most
> — education, health policy, and working conditions — are
> perceived as lying beyond the effective reach of government.
> The challenge is to find a way to bring the core principle of
> democracy — the idea of mutual accountability and non-
> rankist service — to all our social institutions. (Fuller 2003,
> pp. 8-9)

Conventional wisdom informs us that voter participation is
down and cynicism about government is up. Furthermore, it is
conventional wisdom that our democracy suffers when only half
of us vote. But perhaps conventional wisdom is wrong.

Bennett (2003) views such voter turnout as a significant feat,
given what he describes as the "paradox of voting." Bennett's paradox is that all of us know that any one person's vote will have almost
no effect on an election's outcome, thus it is a remarkable testament
to our democracy that about one-half of eligible voters vote in presidential elections. There is no "rational" reason for a person to vote,
and yet nearly one-half of us do. Perhaps looking at the voting paradox as a glass half-full instead of half-empty may be instructive as
we look at the role of public schools in our democracy.

Education institutions transmit cultural norms, including
norms about democracy. However, a number of critics have
denounced both the norms being taught and the system for teaching them. Sanford Levinson writes of the common school that
unintentionally teaches our children to be "value-less, culture-
less, root-less, and religion-less" (2003, p. 205). Gatto argues that
schools have become shills for the corporations:

> Schools are actually laboratories of experimentation on
> young minds, drill centers for the habits and attitudes that
> corporate society demands. Mandatory education serves
> children only incidentally; its real purpose is to turn them
> into servants. (2003, p. 38)

Some believe that the nature of public schooling itself is stifling.
For these critics, an even bigger question than whose cultural
norms are being transmitted lies in the nature of the transmission
process. Gatto (2003) believes that 12-year compulsory school pro-

grams thoroughly bore students and teachers alike. He writes that he came to think of our schools "with their long-term, cell-block style, forced confinement of both students and teachers — as virtual factories of childishness" (p. 34). Gatto points to two million home-schooled children, as well as many of our founding fathers, as evidence that the school routine that we have established may not be necessary. Greer was perhaps among the first of the modern era to question the wisdom of public schooling.

> Once upon a time there was a great nation which became great because of its public schools. That is the American school legend. So the legend supports a social policy which is secure in its faith that the agency for the amelioration of most social problems already exists — and that those problems whose solutions elude us now either will be resolved or are beyond solution, through no fault of that great nation but because of deficiencies in particular people who cannot seem to solve their problems as countless other Americans have before them. It is a pernicious legend, then, because it justifies the exclusion of millions who will never share in America's greatness as long as the legend persists. (Greer 1972, p. 3)

Education for democracy would help put an end to the systems of domination that create the condition we have now, a condition of decidedly unequal influence over who gets what. We presumably need to create an education system in which systemic privilege is no longer a factor. We need to create an education climate in which students have a significant say in their lives.

For all the flaws inherent in public schooling and the necessary implications for social control that flow from universal public schooling, is there a better way to support the common good and sustain the health of American democracy? How might we address civic education and how might we better instill knowledge of and participation in genuine democracy among students?

Public schools continue to be the mainstay of American education. According to Department of Education statistics, approximately 90% of all children in kindergarten through 12th grade attend public schools. Conventional wisdom dictates that the public schools are declining. Whether public schools deserve such criticism is a matter of contentious debate. But it is both ironic and symbolic that the institution blamed for the decline of our democracy has more to do with its ongoing successes and survival than does any other single institution.

Questioning the public schools is an essential part of a thriving democracy. Were we satisfied with our public schools to the point of unquestioned loyalty, we would not be practicing the type of citizenship that we learned within those public schools. It is a conundrum to be sure, and it must surely be the bane of many a public school teacher that they may be doing their best to create new generations of critics. But that is the nature of public education for a lasting and thriving democracy.

References

Apple, M.W. *Official Knowledge: Democratic Education in a Conservative Age*. 2nd ed. New York: Routledge, 2000.

Bennett, R.W. *Talking It Through: Puzzles of American Democracy*. Ithaca, N.Y.: Cornell University Press, 2003.

Bowles, S., and Gintis, H. "Schooling in Capitalist America." In *Education, Inc: Turning Learning into a Business*, edited by A. Kohn and P. Shannon. Portsmouth, N.H.: Heinemann, 2002.

Edelsky, C. "Appendix: Education for Democracy." In *Class Actions: Teaching for Social Justice in Elementary and Middle School*, edited by J. Allen. New York: Teachers College Press, 1999.

Fuller, R.W. *Somebodies and Nobodies: Overcoming the Abuse of Rank*. Gabriola Island, B.C., Canada: New Society Publishers, 2003.

Gatto, J.T. "Against School: How Public Education Cripples Our Kids, and Why." *Harper's* 307 (September 2003): 33-38.

Greer, C. *The Great School Legend: A Revisionist Interpretation of American Public Education*. New York: Basic Books, 1972.

Levinson, S. "Promoting Diversity in the Public Schools: Or, to What Extent Does the Establishment Clause of the First Amendment Hinder the Establishment of More Genuinely Multicultural Schools." In *Constitutional Politics: Essays on Constitution Making, Maintenance, and Change*, edited by S.A. Barber and R.P. George. Princeton, N.J.: Princeton University Press, 2001.

Levinson, S. *Wrestling with Diversity*. Durham, N.C.: Duke University Press, 2003.

TEACHING FOR DEMOCRATIC CITIZENSHIP

PATRICIA K. KUBOW

The relationship of the individual to his or her society is an enduring issue in education, for "schools assume particular responsibilities for developing individuals in ways that are linked to the fulfillment of society's needs" (Kubow and Fossum 2003, pp. 86-87).

People's views about the nature of citizenship have changed over time. Historical and social factors have influenced people's views of what citizenship is or should be. From the beginning of the twentieth century to the Korean War, citizenship education in the United States generally was associated with national pride and loyalty. However, the Vietnam War caused Americans to question the limits of patriotism. Blind commitment to the nation-state was viewed by some as "static," "backward-looking," and "supportive of the status quo" (Stanley and Nelson 1991, p. 110). More recently, terrorism and funding for Homeland Security have brought a resurgence of the older views of citizenship education.

The more traditional view is to interpret citizenship in terms of political participation, such as voting for public officials and vol-

Patricia K. Kubow is an associate professor in Educational Foundations and Inquiry at Bowling Green State University. Her work focuses on comparative and international education and explores the intersections of culture, democracy, and pedagogy.

unteering in one's community. For some social educators, limiting public involvement to voting is "woefully partial — a minor, nonassociative act when set against the interactive, buzzing, and inescapably political practices that define strong democracy and strong democratic citizenship" (Parker 1996, p. 9). For global educators, narrow nationalist ideology is considered dangerous to democracy (Bickmore 1993).

Educators in U.S. schools have been caught between traditional and progressive interpretations of democratic citizenship. Part of the problem is that citizenship education in public schools serves a dual purpose: the development of persons loyal to the nation-state and the development of persons capable of and willing to critically assess their society (Engle and Ochoa 1988). This tension between social conformity and social freedom creates controversy about how students should be educated for democratic citizenship.

Although most educators fall somewhere between these polarized positions, citizenship education in U.S. public schools often is characterized by the divide between those who support a traditional, civic learning approach (where the teacher's role is to help prescribe ways for learners to help in their community) and those who support a progressive, critical education approach (where the teacher's role is to encourage learners to challenge the status quo and inequalities in their communities). However, despite the development of courses in international relations, world affairs, and comparative studies, citizenship education in U.S. public schools consists primarily of knowledge about government structures and administration (Butts 1980).

Engle and Ochoa (1988) argue that socialization — the process of learning about society's traditions, rules, customs, and practices — might not equip students for their roles as citizens. These authors argue that, because culture has the tendency "to reproduce itself with all its rigidities, inconsistencies, and inequities" (p. 14), a process of counter-socialization (that is, independent thinking and social criticism) is needed. In their view, socializing practices cultivate respect for others, while counter-socializing processes help learners critically examine their society to improve it.

The socialization counter-socialization schism has been challenged by Whitson and Stanley (1996), who contend that socialization is learning about society's practices, values, and norms, as well as developing the skills to critique and change those norms if necessary. The authors find it problematic to associate reflection and critique with counter-socialization when an important part of education's socializing role is to foster students' ability to examine and question what they are taught. Gutmann (1987) reminds people who would seek to limit critique and action in schools that "the distinctive virtue of a democratic society [is] that it authorizes citizens to influence how their society reproduces itself" (p. 15). Thus when socialization is understood as teaching students both the norms of society and the reflective skills to critique those norms, it may be a more useful way to view the important role of public education in developing democratic citizens. Rosenau writes:

> the responsibilities of citizenship in these complex times are far more extensive and elaborate than our textbooks, mass media, and civic action groups appear to realize. Indeed, the United States is unlikely to make a thoroughgoing adaptation to the changing circumstances of our evermore interdependent world unless the concept of citizenship to which succeeding generations of students are exposed is brought into line with the choices that greater independence imposes on individuals in all walks of life. (1983, p. 29)

Two possibilities for developing a democratic citizenship that embraces this more critically oriented view of socialization are the practical social competence approach and the deliberation approach. The practical social competence approach to citizenship education, offered by Whitson and Stanley (1996), requires the development of learners' "sociological imagination" (the term was coined by C. Wright Mills in 1959). According to the authors, the sociological imagination is formed when learners interpret their personal affairs in relation to larger historical and social forces, recognize how those forces enhance or limit their opportunities as citizens, and act in ways to improve themselves and their society. Therefore the role of education is to develop practical social competence through critical reflection and attention to the belief systems and to the variety of judgments that individuals "can become more or less competent to make" (Whitson and Stanley 1996, p. 326).

Citizens become less able to make sound judgments in a democracy if their values are treated as givens by the society, that is, if students are taught to embrace those values without the opportunity to examine and question them. Whitson and Stanley (1996) argue that it is this questioning on the part of learners, in a democratic classroom environment created by educators, that leads to affirmation of democratic principles. This means that educators must have faith in the democratic values themselves and confidence that learners, when given the opportunity to question those values, will eventually embrace democratic values for themselves and will act with commitment on those principles. According to Whitson and Stanley, democratic values should not be treated as "a priori given attributes of individuals or societies, to be 'analyzed' and 'clarified,' or to be directly taught, observed, applied, and inculcated" (1996, p. 327). Rather, the authors argue that all values should be regarded as judgments that have formed over time and, therefore, are open to reflection, question, and critique.

The second approach to developing democratic competence is through deliberation. Mathews has asserted that educators cannot respond to public cynicism by telling learners to go and vote. Rather, people must learn "about the politics that comes before voting — the politics that informs voting and continues after the elections are over" (1996, p. 284). The aim of democratic citizenship education, then, is to help students "think publicly" (p. 282). The deliberation approach is designed not only to teach political skills, but to advocate "a way of thinking and knowing that depends on public dialogue" (p. 282). It is through public deliberation, Mathews argues, that public interest is made known and common ground created.

When democratic education ends at student assignments to gather information on particular policy issues and to make classroom presentations on what they found, learners do not have the opportunity to move to the difficult stage — the political stage — where one choice must be made from many options. A deliberation-oriented education is an attempt to push decision making beyond that level. Mathews argues that making decisions "requires dealing with differing estimates of the worth of various proposals for common action. It requires skills in moving from first impressions to more reflective and shared judgments" (1996, p. 275).

Parker has identified three types of deliberation-oriented educators: the first places primary importance on rational negotiation of individual interests; the second seeks to create a strong participatory democracy by allowing learners to think about and discuss controversial public issues; and the third views schools as "sites of social transformation where students are encouraged to uncover cultural and political taken-for-granteds and to contest social forces that, left alone, perpetuate entrenched patterns of domination, thus preventing democratic living" (1996, p. 16). In this way, deliberation becomes a means for engaging learners in a process of "conscious social reproduction" (Gutmann 1987, p. 19).

The type of education students receive will influence their perceptions of what citizenship is and how they exercise that citizenship. Thus educators need to help students wrestle with a host of new realities: interdependence, pluralism, periods of instability, and controversies between nation-state loyalties and global responsibilities. If the role of education is to develop democratic citizens who are able to address these complex realities, then the role of educators is to foster an environment in which learners can experience genuine opportunities for active participation and empowerment (Newell and Davis 1988).

Teachers must strive to model the democratic principles they wish to foster in learners. One way is to create more inclusive classrooms by encouraging learners to take a role in classroom governance and their own learning. When students have opportunities to develop classroom rules and to make decisions that affect their learning, they will feel ownership of the school and a sense that their input is important.

Inclusive democratic classrooms are characterized by an ethic of care, concern, and tolerance for differences and divergent views. Teachers can establish such classrooms by teaching democratic concepts, providing opportunities for team learning, encouraging in-depth discussion of relevant social issues, and helping learners view knowledge as open for examination and critique. Providing students with a rationale for why particular content is chosen and why specific teaching methods are used will encourage learners to ask questions and to reflect on what they are being asked to do. Finally, educators can work to deliberate about shared democratic values with other community members, placing their primary value on safeguarding human dignity, personal worth, and the common good.

Although there are many challenges, there are also great possibilities for schools to play a major role in fostering democratic citizenship. Schools are public spaces for deliberation and dialogue. The common-school experience, characterized by diverse student populations, affords opportunities for students and adults to learn how to work cooperatively and to live democratically. Schools must provide opportunities for students to use their knowledge and to practice democratic skills. As Dewey (1937) argued in the beginning of the twentieth century, "it is not whether the schools shall or shall not influence the course of future social life, but in what direction they shall do so and how." What schools will determine is the kind of citizenship that Americans will have in the twenty-first century.

References

Bickmore, K. "Learning Inclusion/Inclusion in Learning: Citizenship Education for a Pluralistic Society." *Theory and Research in Social Education* 21 (1993): 341-84.

Butts, R.F. *The Revival of Civic Learning: A Rationale for Citizenship Education in American Schools*. New York: Teachers College Press, 1980.

Dewey, J. "Education and Social Change." *The Social Frontier* 3, no. 26 (1937): 235-38.

Engle, S.H., and Ochoa, A. *Education for Democratic Citizenship: Decision Making in the Social Studies.* New York: Teachers College Press, 1988.

Gutmann, A. *Democratic Education.* Princeton, N.J.: Princeton University Press, 1987.

Kubow, P.K., and Fossum, P.R. *Comparative Education: Exploring Issues in International Context.* Upper Saddle River, N.J.: Merrill, Prentice-Hall, 2003.

Mathews, D. "Reviewing and Previewing Civics." In *Educating the Democratic Mind*, edited by W.C. Parker. Albany: State University of New York Press, 1996.

Newell, W.H., and Davis, A.J. "Education for Citizenship: The Role of Progressive Education and Interdisciplinary Studies." *Innovative Higher Education* 13, no. 1 (1988): 27-37.

Parker, W.C. *Educating the Democratic Mind.* Albany: State University of New York Press, 1996.

Rosenau, J.N. "Teaching and Learning in a Transnational World." *Educational Research Quarterly* 8, no. 1 (1983): 29-35.

Stanley, W.B., and Nelson, J.L. "Social Education for Social Transformation." In *Model Learner Outcomes for Social Studies Education*, edited by R.W. Wangen and G. Mammenga. St. Paul: Minnesota Department of Education, 1991.

Whitson, J.A., and Stanley, W.B. "'Re-Minding' Education for Democracy." In *Educating the Democratic Mind*, edited by W.C. Parker. Albany: State University of New York Press, 1996.

CHANGING GOVERNANCE, CHANGING VOICE?
Democratic Representation in Public School Governance

ANN ALLEN

The purpose of universal education in America is to provide all children with the skills and knowledge that will serve them well in a democratic society and, likewise, serve democracy with well-prepared citizens. Public education provides the training ground for citizenship by allowing children to consider and debate perspectives from others who are unlike themselves (Gutmann 1987). Thus public education is a common good because its outcomes affect all citizens in a community, not just the parents and students directly involved in day-to-day schooling (Plank and Boyd 1994; Labaree 2000).

Critics of traditional public school governance wonder whether America's one system of education is the best system for meeting these goals and point to the inequality of opportunity, inaccessible bureaucracies, and inefficient systems of public schooling (Chubb and Moe 1990; Olson 1992; Hess 1999; Finn 2003). In the last decade, reformers have experimented with changes in public school governance that both centralize and decentralize the sys-

Ann Allen is a doctoral candidate in education policy at Michigan State University. Her professional experience includes education research and evaluation, as well as teaching high school and college English. Her doctoral research focuses on governance issues in charter and traditional public schools.

tem (Conley 2003; Boyd 2003; Mintrom 2001, 2003). Efforts to standardize curriculum and assessments are taking place at the same time that market advocates are decentralizing schooling through choice and competition. While scholars have focused on examining the effects of these reforms on student achievement, less is known about how these reforms affect citizen participation in making decisions about schools.

Centralization can remove the direct citizen voice in decisions by placing the responsibility for the community's children in the hands of the state or the federal government. Decentralization may provide more participation from a select group of parents (Mintrom 2003), but it can ignore the community at large (Fiske and Ladd 2000).

This does not mean that the practice of public schooling must remain stagnant. Democratic institutions require ongoing deliberation, examination, and reform; and public schools are no exception. However, reformers must consider how a change in public school governance affects the participation of the citizens it aims to serve.

Such recent federal and state policies as the No Child Left Behind Act of 2001 and the increased role states are playing in financing public schools limit local leaders' control over how education is delivered (Conley 2003). These reforms centralize governance and are the result of pressure from policy makers to increase student performance on standardized tests (Boyd 2003). At the same time, pressure from unsatisfied parents has resulted in such governance reforms as choice and charter schools, which put more control in the hands of parents. Unfortunately, there is very little research that examines how these reforms affect citizen participation in the decisions made about public schools.

Citizens must have a voice and the opportunity to participate in making decisions about their schools. As Benveniste, Carnoy, and Rothstein argue, "Society has an interest in the kind of education that its children receive and this should be an area for debate" (2003, p. 106). Voke, in her argument for greater legitimacy for charter schools, writes that the need for citizen participation goes beyond engaging only school parents and that "All citizens have an important and common interest in educating future citizens" (1999, p. 142). The participants in a major Ford Foundation study identified the following two core tenets of successful public school reform:

> 1. Communities bear both the right and the responsibility to foster and protect quality, equitable educational opportunities for their children. 2. A democratic society provides the tools for constituents to participate in shaping, monitoring, and sustaining the policies and practices of public institutions that affect the lives of communities, families, and individuals. (Hirota and Jacobs 2003, p. 3)

Some scholars argue that citizen engagement in civic life helps maintain a balance of power and builds the kind of trust among citizens that is necessary to produce a common good (Putnam 1993; Dahl 1998; Richardson 2002). Social capital theory posits that the more citizens participate in public matters, the more citizens will support services for the public good. In his study of regional governments in Italy, Putnam (1993) found that communities with high social capital had a higher trust in government and, consequently, government was more effective. Scholars who have studied participation in school governance suggest that citizens tend to be more engaged in community matters as a result of their participation in school decision making (Olin and Fung 2003; Salisbury 1980).

Citizen participation in school decision making can positively affect school outcomes. Olin and Fung (2003) note that the increase in deliberative democracy in Chicago's schools has led to stronger programs for students. In another study of Chicago's school reforms, Bryk and Schneider (2003) found that increased participation by parents and community members led to increased trust and support for school initiatives. Bryk and his colleagues (1999) were even more definite about the positive effects of participation on school outcomes. The authors concluded that the local democratic control instituted through the Chicago reforms resulted in an increased energy for change in school communities across race and income levels. School leadership was responsive to community pressure, and organizational capacity developed in support of school improvement.

The benefits of citizen participation in public school outcomes may be apparent from looking at cases where citizen participation is absent. A lack of citizen voice in public school outcomes could contribute to a system of oppression, as is evident in Benham and Heck's (1998) account of Hawaii's public school system, which is the only school system in the nation governed entirely through a single, statewide school board. Likewise, market approaches to education that do not make room for adequate citizen participation can lead to segregation (Miller-Kahn and Smith 2001) or elitism that provides benefits for some at the expense of benefits for all (Fiske and Ladd 2000).

It is right to consider reforming school governance, but changing governance can change voice. A careful consideration of how today's governance reforms affect citizen voice and participation in school decision making will help illuminate the effect of these reforms on the democratic nature of public schools.

Mintrom's (2003) study on parent participation in charter schools concludes that charter school administrators solicit more parental input in school decisions than do administrators in traditional public schools. However, Benveniste, Carnoy, and Rothstein (2003), in their comparison of private and public schools, indicate that parental voice in charter schools is less democratic and less deliberative than parental voice in traditionally governed public schools because parents in charter schools, like those in private schools, are more accountable to school authority. Based on these competing conclusions, there is some question as to what makes for democratic deliberation in school decision making.

The elements of democratic representation outlined below stem from work aimed at strengthening democratic structures in American society (Plank and Boyd 1994; Gutmann 1987; Dahl 1998; Williams 1998; Richardson 2002; Hirota and Jacobs 2003). These elements provide a framework for analyzing the practice of democratic voice. In their report to the Ford Foundation, Hirota and Jacobs (2003) identified democratic structures important to citizen voice as: the right of assembly, representation, freedom of speech, access to information, and the use of the courts and elections. Dahl's (1998) description of the basic structures of democratic representation is similar, but it includes a provision for inclusive citizenship and free, fair, and frequent elections. Specifically, Dahl identified structures of democratic representation as: elected officials; free, fair, and frequent elections; freedom of expression; access to alternative sources of information; associational autonomy; and inclusive citizenship. The basic elements of democratic representation described by Dahl and others provide a framework with which to analyze the public nature of today's education governance reforms.

Choice in Representation. By electing officials, citizens delegate the authority for decision making to a few representatives who act on behalf of the citizens they serve. It can be argued that as the size of the school community gets smaller, the need for representation is less because, theoretically, more people have the ability to participate without elected representatives. Creating smaller organizations with closer ties to the people they serve was one of the motivations behind the charter school reforms (Chubb and Moe 1990) and one of the arguments behind the current call to do away with local school boards (Finn 2003). However, as Voke (1999) points out, public charter schools serve more than just the parents and students in the school; they also serve nonparent community members. Dahl (1998) argues that organizations that serve multiple constituencies with multiple interests require a system of democratic representation because no one person is likely to ensure consideration of all interests and goals.

How representatives are chosen can affect the nature of representation in school decisions. Critics of appointed boards argue that appointments result in less democracy because voters do not directly choose their own representations. Schools with appointed boards, such as charter schools or schools controlled by mayors or governors, receive authority from the state's elected governor and legislature. Bryk et al. (1999) note that the mayoral appointments made to the school board in Chicago very closely reflected the political ideology of the mayor. The question of appointed boards then becomes: Whose interests do appointed boards represent?

Formal election processes do not automatically ensure fair and equal representation. Progressive-era reformers, in an effort to de-politicize education, established school elections separately from general municipal elections, which resulted in separate elections for the majority of public school issues (Tyack 1974). While the structure of school elections effectively separates school issues from other issues and takes the school election out of the partisan political arena, voter turnout in these special elections is very low. Lutz and Iannacone (1978) suggest that the voters who show up for these elections are not representative of the entire population. Meier (2002) calls such elections quiet, untimely elections that serve to control citizens' voice in public school governance issues.

Freedom of Expression. Whose voice is heard is an important consideration in all methods of deliberation. Dahl (1998) argues that freedom of expression by all citizens is necessary for effective participation. Citizens must be able to express themselves freely and they must be able to listen to others' expressions in order to learn about and deliberate on possible actions.

Gutmann (1987) offers a design for deliberation in public schools that requires a certain level of skill and knowledge to be able to engage in civic debates. She calls for an increased attention to democratic education that is nonrepressive and nondiscriminatory in order to develop citizens capable of such debate. Critics of deliberation argue that deliberation far too often serves only the voices of those who are already empowered (Williams 1998) and that strict deliberative democracy is ineffective in achieving outcomes (Posner 2003). However, even these critics concede that there is a role in representative democracy for expression of citizens' ideas and that deliberation in moderation can serve to enrich, not derail, decisions on policy outcomes.

How governance reforms are established and implemented can affect the freedom of voice in school decision making. The contrasting conclusions that Mintrom (2003) and Benveniste and his colleagues (2003) draw regarding the deliberative nature of parental voice in decisions in charter schools is a case in point. Parental voice may be solicited more in such smaller organizations as charter schools, but it may be solicited in a way that aims to promote or protect the charter school's status (Benveniste et al. 2003). Governance reforms should be assessed on their tendencies to inhibit or encourage the free expression of citizen voice.

Access to Information. Dahl argues that effective participation depends on citizens' ability to access alternative and independent sources of information. Public schools are subject to freedom of information laws that make nearly all information of public concern available to citizens by request. However, in their evaluation of Michigan's charter schools, Miron and Nelson (2002) present evidence that some charter schools — because of contracts with private management companies or education management organizations — have kept some of this information private. Private companies can control information about charter schools as the property of the private organization and not as public information for citizen review. Governance reforms that place private organizations in charge of public schools may affect the access citizens have to information about those public schools.

Associational Representation. One critique of democratic representation is that it often does not serve the underrepresented, and there are citizens who cannot effectively represent themselves even when given the opportunity. Dahl (1998) argues for independent associations as part of the democratic structure in order to help citizens with similar issues to express their concerns. Dahl also contends that independent associations increase civic enlightenment by providing citizens with information and education. Williams (1998) advocates for the use of associational representation as a means for underrepresented voices to be heard.

One benefit of the market reform is that it allows parents to make choices based on their interests, resulting in services for like-minded people (Hess 2003). Smith (1999) argues that charter schools provide associational representation by serving groups of students who have similar needs. However, Voke (1999) contends that this view of representation is faulty because it does not consider the interests or voices of nonparent citizens.

Inclusion. Choice reforms attempt to increase parents' voice in making school decisions by simplifying the organizational barriers to voice. Charter school reformers create cultures that like-minded parents and students join (Miller-Kahn and Smith 2001; Lubienski 2003). However, the governance system of autonomous charter schools can isolate the charter school community, including only the parents, students, and educators in the school but excluding the rest of the community. While Mintrom (2003) and Benveniste and his colleagues (2003) have begun to look at the effect of school governance reform on parental voice, neither study addresses what opportunities may be available to nonparents for deliberating on decisions in charter schools.

Public education is a complex web of goals, interests, and constituencies because its outcomes affect all citizens in a community (Labaree 1997, 2000). Reaching some consensus on the "ultimate agenda" (Dahl 1998) of schooling in such an environment depends on an ability to address those varied interests. How governance reforms are defined and implemented can determine whose voice is considered in school decisions.

The traditional governance of public schooling has relied on locally elected school boards to serve as representatives of the community. However, traditional public school governance systems are facing increasing criticism for being ineffective modes for accountability and barriers to school improvement. In addition, it is not clear that traditional school governance, in practice, meets the requirements of democratic representation. It is not a foregone conclusion that the problem with American education is too much democracy. It is very possible that the problem is that American education governance is not democratic enough.

Governance reforms that eliminate citizen voice and participation in making decisions about schools may make it easier to implement reforms, but for whose interests and to what end? While it may be that there are some institutions in a democratic society that are small or simple enough that one person can ensure equal consideration of all citizens, it is not likely that public education is one of them. The complexity of public schooling requires citizen participation in making decisions in order to effectively consider the multiple goals and interests of the school constituency and to provide citizens an opportunity to examine and challenge the balance of those goals.

It is clear that governance matters, for better or worse. Education reformers are looking for ways to reconstitute school governance so that it matters for the better. Citizen participation and voice in school decisions are important and necessary aspects of governance in a democratic system of public schooling.

A public education system that serves the common good is fundamental for a democratic society. However, it is impossible to define what is common about our lives without a clear and comprehensive representation of citizen voice. We cannot continue to move forward with large-scale governance reforms, such as charter schools, take-overs, or such federal mandates as No Child Left Behind, without considering more carefully their effect on the democratic representation of all citizens.

References

Benham, M., and Heck, R.H. *Culture and Educational Policy in Hawaii: The Silencing of Native Voices.* New York: Basic Books, 1998.

Benveniste, L.; Carnoy, M.; and Rothstein, R. *All Else Equal: Are Public and Private Schools Different?* New York: Routledge Falmer, 2003.

Boyd, W.L. "Public Education's Crisis of Performance and Legitimacy: Introduction and Overview of the Yearbook." In *American Governance on Trial: Change and Challenges,* edited by W.L. Boyd. National Society for the Study of Education Yearbook. Chicago: University of Chicago Press, 2003.

Bryk, A., and Schneider, B. "Trust in Schools: A Core Resource for School Reform." *Educational Leadership* 60, no. 6 (2003): 40-45.

Bryk, A.S.; Sebring, P.B.; Kerbow, D.; Rollow, S.; and Easton, J.Q. *Charting Chicago School Reform: Democratic Localism as a Lever for Change.* Boulder, Colo.: Westview, 1999.

Chubb, J.E., and Moe, T.M. *Politics, Markets and America's Schools.* Washington, D.C.: Brookings Institution, 1990.

Conley, D. *Who Governs Our Schools: Changing Roles and Responsibilities.* New York: Teachers College Press, 2003.

Dahl, R.A. *On Democracy.* New Haven, Conn.: Yale University Press, 1998.

Finn, C. "Reinventing Local Control." *Education Week*, 23 January 1991, pp. 32, 40.

Finn, C. "Who Needs School Boards?" *The Education Gadfly*, 23 October 2003. Thomas Fordham Foundation. www.edexcellence. net/foundation/gadfly/issue.cfm?id=120#1505

Fiske, E.B., and Ladd, H.F. *When Schools Compete: A Cautionary Tale.* Washington D.C.: Brookings Institution, 2000.

Gutmann, A. *Democratic Education.* Princeton, N.J.: Princeton University Press, 1987.

Hess, F.M. *Spinning Wheels: The Politics of Urban School Reform.* Washington, D.C.: Brookings Institution, 1999.

Hess, F.M. "Breaking the Mold: Charter Schools, Contract Schools, and Voucher Plans." In *American Governance on Trial: Change and Challenges*, edited by W.L. Boyd. National Society for the Study of Education Yearbook. Chicago: University of Chicago Press, 2003.

Hill, P.T. "How to Fix the Educational Governance System." In *American Governance on Trial: Change and Challenges*, edited by W.L. Boyd. National Society for the Study of Education Yearbook. Chicago: University of Chicago Press, 2003.

Hirota, J.M., and Jacobs, L.E. *Vital Voices: Building Constituencies for Public School Reform. A Report to the Ford Foundation.* New York: Academy for Educational Development, Chapin Hill Center for Children, 2003.

Labaree, D.F. "Public Goods, Private Goods: The American Struggle Over Educational Goals." *American Educational Research Journal* 34 (Spring 1997): 39-81.

Labaree, D.F. "Resisting Educational Standards." *Phi Delta Kappan* 82 (September 2000): 28-33.

Land, D. "Local School Boards Under Review." *Review of Education Research* 72 (Summer 2002): 229-78.

Lipsky, M. *Street Level Bureaucracy: Dilemmas of the Individual in Public Services.* New York: Russell Sage Foundation, 1983.

Lubienski, C. "School Competition and Promotion: Substantive and Symbolic Differences in Local Education Markets." *Occasional Paper No. 80.* New York: Columbia University, National Center for the Study of Privatization in Education, 2003. www.ncspe.org

Lutz, F., and Innaconne, L. *Public Participation in School Decision Making.* Lexington, Mass.: Lexington Books, 1978.

Meier, K. "A Research Agenda on Elections and Education." *Educational Policy* 16, no. 1 (2002): 219-30.

Miller-Kahn, L., and Smith, M.L. "School Choice Policies in the Political Spectacle." *Education Policy Analysis Archives* 9 (November 2001). epaa.asu.edu.

Mintrom, M. "Educational Governance and Democratic Practice." *Educational Policy* 15 (November 2001): 615-43.

Mintrom, M. "Market Organizations and Deliberative Democracy: Choice and Voice in Public Service Delivery." *Administration & Society* 35 (March 2003): 52-81.

Miron, G., and Nelson, C. *What's Public About Charter Schools: Lessons Learned About Choice and Accountability.* Thousand Oaks, Calif.: Corwin, 2002.

Olin, E., and Fung, A. *Deepening Democracy: Institutional Innovations in Empowered Participatory Governance. The Real Utopia Project IV.* New York: Verso, 2003.

Olson, L. "Boards of Contention." *Education Week,* 29 April 1992, pp. 23-25, 27, 28.

Plank, D.N., and Boyd, W.H. "Antipolitics, Education and Institutional Choice: The Flight from Democracy." *American Educational Research Journal* 31, no. 2 (1994): 263-81.

Posner, R.A. *Law, Pragmatism, and Democracy.* Cambridge, Mass.: Harvard University Press, 2003.

Putnam, R. *Making Democracy Work: Civic Traditions in Modern Italy.* Princeton, N.J.: Princeton University Press, 1993.

Richardson, H.S. *Democratic Autonomy: Public Reasoning About the Ends of Policy.* New York: Oxford University Press, 2002.

Salisbury, R.H. *Citizen Participation in the Public Schools.* Lexington, Ky.: Lexington Books, 1980.

Smith, S. "Charter Schools: Voluntary Associations or Political Communities?" In *Philosophy of Education 1998*, edited by Steven Tozer. Urbana, Ill.: Philosophy of Education Society, 1999.

Tyack, D. *The One Best System: A History of American Urban Education*. Cambridge, Mass.: Harvard University Press, 1974.

Voke, H.M. "Charter Schools: Particularistic, Pluralistic, and Participatory?" In *Philosophy of Education 1998*, edited by Steven Tozer. Urbana, Ill.: Philosophy of Education Society, 1999.

Williams, M. *Voice, Trust and Memory: Marginalized Groups and the Failings of Liberal Representation*. Princeton, N.J.: Princeton University Press, 1998.

TEACHING FOR WISDOM: What Matters Is Not What Students Know, But How They Use It

Robert J. Sternberg

A few days ago, my wife and I were on our way to an important meeting but got stuck in a maddening traffic jam. As we approached an exit along our slow, bumpy, and obstacle-laden route, we noted that the highway that extended out from the exit, which was perpendicular to the direction in which we were going, was wonderfully paved and the traffic was moving rapidly with no obstacles along its course. We actually talked about taking that route. There was only one problem: The route led nowhere we wanted or needed to go, nor where we should have gone. Nevertheless, it was just so tempting.

Although my wife and I did not take that route, the U.S. education system has. I believe it is going rapidly and relatively smoothly — in the wrong direction. That wrong direction is illustrated by the system of high-stakes testing that has come to dominate the country. It is not that high-stakes testing is, in itself, necessarily bad. It is that what the tests measure, to a large extent, doesn't

Robert J. Sternberg is IBM Professor of Psychology and Education and director of the Center for the Psychology of Abilities, Competencies, and Expertise at Yale University. Preparation of this article was supported by a grant from the W.T. Grant Foundation. Grantees undertaking such projects are encouraged to express freely their professional judgment. This article, therefore, does not necessarily represent the positions or the policies of the W. T. Grant Foundation.

matter all that much in the long run. What matters is not only *how much* knowledge you have, but how you *use* that knowledge — whether for good ends (as Mahatma Gandhi or Martin Luther King Jr.) or for bad ones (as Adolph Hitler and Joseph Stalin). What has distinguished wise leaders from foolish ones is not how much they knew, but how they used what they knew and whether they used it to foster a democratic ideal and a common good or a totalitarian society good for only the dictator and his cronies.

Many societies today are preoccupied with the development of knowledge and basic cognitive skills in school children. But are knowledge and basic cognitive skills — the essential ingredients of intelligence as classically defined — enough? Consider the following.

Flynn (1998) has pointed out that in more than a dozen other countries for which records have been available, IQs have been rising at a rate of roughly nine points per generation (30 years). This increase has been going on for at least several generations (see also Neisser 1998).

With IQs going up and IQ-related abilities counting more and more for success in the society, one can only conclude that the IQ-like abilities of those at the top of the socioeconomic spectrum are higher than ever before — even higher than would be predicted merely by the Flynn effect. After all, IQs have become more important for gaining access to higher education and premium jobs. But again, the rise in IQs among the socioeconomic elite does not seem to have created a happier or more harmonious society, and one only has to read the daily newspapers to see the poor uses to which high IQ can be put. Judging by the amount, seriousness, and sheer scale of global conflict, perhaps not much of the increase in IQ is going to creating a common good. Certainly there is no reason to believe that increasing IQs have improved people's or nations' relations with each other. Indeed, today there is more terrorism than at any time in recent memory. In the 1990s, there were more genocides and massacres than at any time since World War II. As people became smarter, they became, if anything, less wise and moved further from, rather than closer to, the pursuit of a common good. There seems to be more hate in the world now than ever before (Sternberg 2003).

The memory and analytical skills that are so central to intelligence are certainly important for school and life success, but perhaps they are not sufficient. One can be smart but foolish. We have seen this in political leaders and in business leaders, such as at Enron, Arthur Andersen, WorldCom, and elsewhere. Smart but foolish people are susceptible to one or more of five fallacies (Sternberg 2002):

- *Unrealistic optimism:* They believe that they are so smart that whatever they do will work out just fine, regardless of whether it really makes sense.
- *Egocentrism:* They start to view decisions only in terms of how the decisions benefit them.
- *Omniscience:* They think that they are all-knowing; they don't know what they don't know.
- *Omnipotence:* They think that they can do whatever they want.
- *Invulnerability:* They think that they are so smart that they can get away with anything they do.

Students and teachers alike need to realize that fallacies such as these are not just mistakes "other people" make. We all are susceptible to foolish thinking. Indeed, the "smarter" we are, the more we may think ourselves immune to foolishness. And it is this fantasy that we are immune that makes us all the more susceptible.

Arguably, wisdom-related skills are at least as important as, or even more important than, sheer knowledge and intelligence.

What Is Wisdom?

Wisdom can be defined as the "power of judging rightly and following the soundest course of action, based on knowledge, experience, understanding, etc." (*Webster's New World College Dictionary* 1997, p. 1533). A number of psychologists have attempted to understand wisdom in more variegated ways. The approaches underlying some of these attempts are summarized in Sternberg (1990, 1998*a*), and Sternberg and Jordan (in press). It is beyond the scope of this article to review all of these different approaches.

Wisdom is defined here as the application of intelligence, creativity, and knowledge as mediated by values toward the achievement of a common good through a balance among: a) intrapersonal, b) interpersonal, and c) extrapersonal interests over both the short and the long term. This application is to achieve a balance among: a) adaptation to existing environments, b) shaping of existing environments, and c) selection of new environments (Sternberg 1998a, 2001), as shown in Figure 1.

Thus wisdom is not just about maximizing one's own or someone else's self-interest, but about balancing various self-interests (intrapersonal) with the interests of others (interpersonal) and with the context in which one lives (extrapersonal), such as one's city or country or environment or even God.

An implication of this view is that when one applies intelligence, creativity, and knowledge, one may deliberately seek outcomes that are good for oneself and bad for others. In wisdom, however, one certainly may seek good ends for oneself, but one also seeks common good outcomes for others. If one's motivations are to maximize certain people's interests and minimize other people's, wisdom is not involved. In wisdom, one seeks a common good, realizing that this common good may be better for some than for others.

I refer here to "interests," which are related to the multiple points of view that are a common feature of many theories of wisdom (as reviewed in Sternberg 1990). Diverse interests encompass multiple points of view, and thus the use of the term *interests* is intended to include "points of view." Sometimes differences in points of view derive not so much from differences in cognitions as from differences in motivations, as when teachers and boards of education have different ideas about how scarce budget dollars should be spent.

Problems requiring wisdom always involve at least some element of intrapersonal, interpersonal, and extrapersonal interests. For example, one might decide that it is wise to take a particular

Figure 1. Wisdom as tacit knowledge balancing goals, responses, and interests.

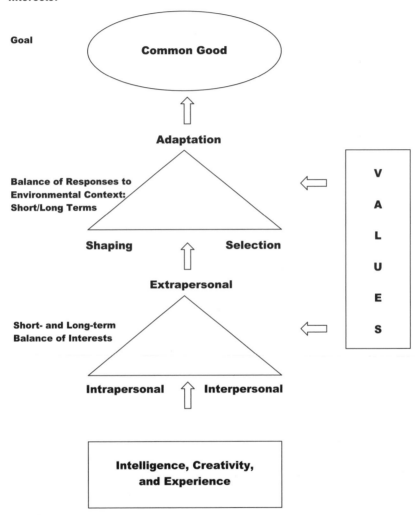

teaching position, a decision that seemingly involves only one person. But many people typically are affected by an individual's decision to take a job — significant others, children, perhaps parents and friends. And the decision always has to be made in the context of the whole range of available options. Similarly, a decision about whether to increase the importance of high-stakes testing requires wisdom because it involves the people who take the tests, their parents, their schools, and the society.

Wisdom involves balancing not only the three kinds of interests but also three possible courses of action in response to this balancing: adaptation of oneself or others to existing environments, shaping of environments in order to render them more compatible with oneself or others, and selection of new environments (Sternberg 1985, 1997). In adaptation, the individual tries to find ways to conform to the existing environment that forms his or her context. Sometimes adaptation is the best course of action under a given set of circumstances. But typically one seeks a balance between adaptation and shaping, realizing that fitting to an environment requires not only changing oneself but also changing the environment. When an individual finds it impossible or at least implausible to attain such a fit, he or she may decide to select a new environment altogether, leaving, for example, a job, a community, a marriage, or whatever.

Wise thinking will not develop simply by teaching for other kinds of thinking. How might it be nurtured? And why is it so scarce?

Implications for Education

My speculation is that increases in intelligence — at least as measured by IQ — have not been matched by comparable increases in wisdom. Indeed, to the extent that our society has increasingly stressed the use of IQ to maximize one's own chances of admission to and success in the "cognitive elite" posited by Herrnstein and Murray (1994), increases in IQ may have been concomitant with decreases in wisdom. High IQ with a scarcity of wisdom has bought us a world with the power to finish itself off many times over.

Wisdom might bring us a world that would seek instead to better itself and the conditions of the people in it. At some level, we as a society have a choice. What do we wish to maximize through our schooling? Is it only knowledge? Is it only intelligence? Or is it knowledge, intelligence, and wisdom? If it also is wisdom, then we need to put our students on a much different course. We need to value not only how they use their outstanding individual abilities to maximize their attainments but also how they use their individual abilities to maximize the attainments of others. We need, in short, to value wisdom.

What would education look like that valued wisdom? Consider the principles we are using in our own course for developing wisdom, which is infused into middle-school American history: Principles of teaching for wisdom derived from the Balance Theory of Wisdom.

Teachers who teach for wisdom will explore with students the notion that conventional abilities and achievements are not enough for a satisfying life. Many people become trapped in their lives and, despite feeling conventionally successful, feel that their lives lack fulfillment. Fulfillment is not an alternative to success. Rather, it is an aspect of it that, for most people, goes beyond money, promotions, large houses, and so forth. The teacher will further demonstrate how wisdom is critical for a satisfying life. In the long run, wise decisions benefit people in ways that foolish decisions never do. The teacher must teach students the usefulness of interdependence — a rising tide raises all ships; a falling tide can sink them.

It also is important to model wisdom, because what you do is more important than what you say. Students should read about wise judgments and making decisions in the context of the actions that follow so that they understand that such means of judging and making decisions exist. Teachers need to help students learn to recognize their own interests, those of other people, and those of institutions. They further need to help students learn to *balance* their own interests, those of other people, and those of institutions. They will teach students that the means by which an end is obtained matters, not just the end. Students need to be encouraged to form, critique, and integrate their values in their thinking. They need to learn to think *dialectically* (Hegel 1931), realizing that both questions and answers evolve over time, and that the answer to an important life question can differ at various times in one's life. Wisdom further requires students to learn to think *dialogically*, whereby they understand interests and ideas from multiple viewpoints. For example, what one group views as a "settler," another may view as an "invader." Most important, students need to learn to search for and then try to reach the common good — a good where everyone wins.

Teaching for wisdom will succeed only if teachers encourage and reward wisdom. Teachers must make wisdom real for students' lives. They should teach students to monitor events in their lives and their thought processes about these events. One way to learn to recognize others' interests is to begin to identify your own. They also should help students understand the importance of inoculating oneself against the pressures of unbalanced self-interest and small-group interest.

Students will develop wisdom by becoming engaged in class discussions, projects, and essays that encourage them to discuss the lessons they have learned from both classical and modern works and how these lessons can be applied to their own lives and the lives of others. They need to study not only "truth," as we know it, but values. The idea is not to force-feed a set of values, but to encourage students to develop their own.

A teacher role model of wisdom will, I believe, take a much more Socratic approach to teaching than teachers customarily do. Students often want large quantities of information spoon-fed or even force-fed to them. They then attempt to memorize this material for exams, only to forget it soon after. In a wisdom-based approach to teaching, students need to take a more active role in constructing their learning. But a wisdom-based approach is not, in my view, tantamount to a constructivist approach to learning. Students have not achieved or even come close to achieving wisdom when they merely have constructed their own learning. Rather, they must be able to construct knowledge not only from their own point of view but also to reconstruct it from the point of view of others. Constructivism from only a single point of view can lead to egocentric, rather than balanced, understanding.

Lessons taught to emphasize wisdom would have a rather different character from lessons as they often are taught today. Social studies and especially history lessons would look very different.

For example, high school American history books typically teach American history from only one point of view, that of the new Americans. Thus Columbus is referred to as having "discovered" America, a strange notion from the standpoint of the many who already lived on the continent when Columbus arrived. The conquest of the Southwest and the Alamo also are presented from the point of view of the new settlers, not also from the standpoint of, say, the Mexicans who lost roughly half their territory. This kind of American ethnocentric and frankly propagandistic teaching would have no place in a curriculum that sought to develop wisdom and an appreciation of the need to balance interests.

Second, science teaching would no longer be about facts presented as though they are the final word. Science often is presented as though it represents the end point of a process of evolution of thought, rather than one of many midpoints (Sternberg 1998b). Students could scarcely realize from this kind of teaching that the paradigms of today, and thus the theories and findings that emanate from them, will eventually be superseded, much as the paradigms, theories, and findings of yesterday were replaced by those of today. Students further need to learn that, contrary to the way many textbooks are written, the classical "scientific method" is largely a fantasy, and scientists are as susceptible to fads as are members of other groups.

Third, the teaching of literature needs to reflect a kind of balance that now is usually absent. Literature often is taught in terms of the standards and contexts of the contemporary U.S. scene. Characters are judged in terms of our standards, rather than the standards of the time and place in which the events took place. From the proposed standpoint, the study of literature must, to some extent, be done in the context of the study of history. The banning of books often reflects the application of certain contemporary standards to literature, standards of which an author from the past never could have been aware.

Fourth, foreign languages always would be taught in the cultural context in which they are embedded. I suggest that American students have so much more difficulty learning foreign languages than do children in much of Europe not because they lack the ability but because they lack the motivation. They do not see the need to learn another language, whereas, say, a Flemish-speaking child in Belgium does. Americans would be better off, I suggest, if they made more of an attempt to understand other cultures, rather than just expect people from other cultures to understand them. Learning the language of a culture is a key to understanding. Americans might be less quick to impose their cultural values on others if they understood the others' cultural values. It is also interesting to speculate on why Esperanto, a language that was to provide a common medium of communication across cultures, has been a notable failure. I suggest that it is because Esperanto is embedded in no culture at all. It is the native language of no one.

Culture cannot be taught, in the context of foreign-language learning, in the way it now often is — as an aside divorced from the actual learning of the language. It should be taught as an integral part of the language — as a primary context in which the language is embedded. The vituperative fights we see about bilingual education and about use of Spanish in the United States or French in Canada are not fights only about language. They are fights about culture, and they are fights in need of wise resolutions.

Finally, as implied throughout these examples, the curriculum needs to be far more integrated. Literature needs to be integrated with history, science with history and social-policy studies, foreign language with culture. Even within disciplines, far more integration is needed.

The road to this new approach is bound to be a rocky one. First, entrenched structures, whatever they may be, are difficult to change; and wisdom neither is taught in schools nor, in general, is it even discussed. Second, many people will not see the value of teaching something that shows no promise of raising conventional test scores. These scores, which formerly were predictors of more interesting criteria, have now become criteria, or ends in themselves. The society has lost track of why they ever mattered in the first place, and they have engendered the same kind of mindless competition we see in people who relentlessly compare their economic achievements with those of others. Third, wisdom is much more difficult to develop than is the kind of achievement that can be developed and then readily tested by multiple-choice tests. Finally, people who have gained influence and power in a society by one means are unlikely to want either to give up that power or to see new criteria established on which they do not rank as favorably.

There is no easy road to wisdom. There never was and probably never will be. As an education system, we have turned on the easy road but the wrong road. It is not too late to turn back. By ratcheting up our emphasis on a narrow conception of what it means to be a "good student," we are ignoring the broader conception that will make a difference to individuals and society. It is not merely what we know but how we use it that will determine the fate of our society and of others.

References

Flynn, J.R. "IQ Gains over Time: Toward Finding the Causes." In *The Rising Curve: Long-Term Gains in IQ and Related Measures*, edited by U. Neisser. Washington, D.C.: American Psychological Association, 1998.

Hegel, G.W.F. *The Phenomenology of the Mind*. 2nd ed. J. D. Baillie, trans. London: Allen and Unwin, 1931. (Original work published 1807.)

Herrnstein, R.J., and Murray, C. *The Bell Curve*. New York: Free Press, 1994.

Neisser, U. *The Rising Curve: Long-Term Gains in IQ and Related Measures*. Washington, D.C.: American Psychological Association, 1998.

Sternberg, R.J. *Beyond IQ: A Triarchic Theory of Human Intelligence*. New York: Cambridge University Press, 1985.

Sternberg, R.J., ed. *Wisdom: Its Nature, Origins, and Development*. New York: Cambridge University Press, 1990.

Sternberg, R.J. *Successful Intelligence*. New York: Plume, 1997.

Sternberg, R.J. "A Balance Theory of Wisdom." *Review of General Psychology* 2 (1998): 347-65. a

Sternberg, R.J. "The Dialectic as a Tool for Teaching Psychology." *Teaching of Psychology* 25 (1998): 177-80. b

Sternberg, R.J. "Why Schools Should Teach for Wisdom: The Balance Theory of Wisdom in Educational Settings." *Educational Psychologist* 36, no. 4 (2001): 227-45.

Sternberg, R.J., ed. *Why Smart People Can Be So Stupid*. New Haven, Conn.: Yale University Press, 2002.

Sternberg, R.J. "A Duplex Theory of Hate: Development and Application to Terrorism, Massacres, and Genocide." *Review of General Psychology* 7, no. 3 (2003): 299-328.

Sternberg, R.J., and Jordan, J. *Handbook of Wisdom: Psychological Perspectives.* New York: Cambridge University Press, in press.

Webster's New World Dictionary. 3rd ed. New York: Simon and Schuster, 1997.

CHILDREN OF PROMISE

MARY ANN MANOS

Many people know that Thomas Jefferson called for the United States to educate all of its citizens. He argued that literacy is essential for the continuance of a democratic society and that state governments must take the financial responsibility to provide a general education for young citizens. Fewer people know that he went further to recommend the identification, through rigorous examination, of those children who have "the best and most promising genius" and to advance such gifted children beyond their peers.

Such thinking is out of style with egalitarian views in American public schools in the 21st century. Our modern democratic practice is to lump all students together (Simon 1996). Many modern American educators bristle at the very thought of identifying a student as "the best" or "a promising genius." They argue that it is too "elitist" or too "separatist" to believe that certain children are endowed with a higher cognitive ability or are more talented than their classmates.

Mary Ann Manos is an associate professor in the College of Education and Health Science at Bradley University, where she is director of the Institute for Talented and Gifted Youth. A graduate of the University of Texas at Austin, Manos was a classroom teacher for 30 years and holds a certification by the National Board for Professional Teaching Standards. Manos is the author of several professional books and articles.

The unfortunate result is that many American students who demonstrate advanced levels of cognition or exceptional talent remain educationally malnourished in today's public schools. We are wasting our nation's intellectual capital.

Can we afford, as a nation, to be equal in all things? Equality indicates sameness in distribution of resources and the meting out of opportunity. For American schools, this benign sameness implies that students are identical in their learning needs if they are working at grade level. On the other hand, if the student is "at-risk" or learning below grade level, more opportunity for instructional support is expected and provided. This duality becomes cancerous for those students who are working well above their grade placement. Such students rarely have the opportunity to receive instruction that challenges them, to be provided with resources that enhance their learning, or to have education experts design and implement exciting instruction for them. To ensure true opportunity, school programs and curricular offerings must provide each student with the opportunity to develop fully their individual potential. Schools that fail in this critical mission plant the seeds of failure for highly able students. What is the result?

Shamus knows the result. Shamus, a five-year-old kindergarten student, attends public school near his home. Shamus is a highly gifted child. He easily reads and comprehends at the sixth-grade level. But there is no high-ability class offered in his school district. As a result, Shamus, with his classmates, will sing the alphabet song again and again. Today, Shamus will be coloring the letter "L" on several primary worksheets, rather than reading the "L" volume of the children's encyclopedia. Daily, he is doomed to do school work six years *below* his ability level. Eventually, he will give up trying. It will not take very long.

Shamus has inherited years of neglect in gifted education. Three decades of federal and state reform have resulted in expanded educational opportunity and protection for American disabled students, homeless children, gender and minority groups, and at-risk students. During this same time, gifted education programs in our nation's elementary schools have experienced neglect and austerity. Of every $100 in federal funds spent on education, less than 2¢ is targeted for gifted education (Karnes and Marquardt 2000). Gifted children are expected to do quite well with very little: no classroom modifications, no specialized learning environment, no qualified teacher, and little challenging curriculum.

Who are these so-called "gifted" students? Where are they found?

The definition of "gifted" is a matter of ongoing and intense debate. No single definition has been accepted by education or government institutions. There is not even agreement on what to call such children, and a gifted child may be called many things: superior, gifted, mentally gifted, high-ability, academically advanced, talented, high-achiever, highly gifted, and rapid learner.

More important, highly able students come from every socio-economic level. Lewis Terman (1920-1950) expected 1% to 3% of the general school population to be highly gifted, representatives of a super-cognition group who would lead academics at the national level (Heller, Monks, and Paslow 1993). The Marland Report (1972) suggested 3% to 5% of the general school population to be identified as gifted. The work of Joseph Renzulli continues to expand the definition of the gifted child as a child who shows above-average ability and highly creative thinking, as well as strong task determination. Renzulli describes a student who is a remarkable combination of talent, perseverance, and "out of the box" ideas; and his definition suggests that 15% to 20% of the school population will exhibit giftedness. All proponents of gifted education describe students from the general school population, from every racial group, and from every income level.

High-ability children, especially those in poverty, have lost important educational opportunities because gifted programs continue to be excluded from federal and state funding (Ford and Russo 1995). Thus states have looked to leadership from the U.S. Department of Education.

Throughout the past 30 years, federal recommendations for gifted education have been prolific. Beginning with the National

Defense Education Act in 1958, schools were expected to identify students who showed great promise in math and science. Such students were considered essential talent to enhance national success in the space race. In 1972 Sidney Marland, then U.S. Commissioner of Education, presented a report to Congress that advocated identification of gifted students and noted they will require services or activities not ordinarily provided by the school. Another benchmark in both federal definition and identification of gifted students came in 1988 with the Jacob Jarvits Gifted and Talented Student Act. And in 1993 the U.S. Department of Education report, *National Excellence: A Case for Developing America's Talent*, expanded the definition of gifted students to include those who show potential for high-levels of intellectual, creative, or artistic performance or unusual leadership capacity.

Unfortunately, no federal mandates exist to fund gifted education on a level comparable with funding for special education. The landmarks in special education – The Rehabilitation Act of 1973, P.L. 94-142 (1975), and I.D.E.A. (1990) – provide some shelter for gifted programs in states that wish to include gifted education as special education programs. Currently, the federal government does not provide adequate funding for gifted education, nor are states expected to mandate local funding. Local control has brought a hodge-podge of programs, many of which exist in a school for only one or two years.

Today, school funds are stretched to cover special education and other essentials. All of the factors affecting education have focused on students who are deemed the most at risk. This has placed gifted children last in line for federal, state, and local support or encouragement.

Skeptics pose the question: Why offer any gifted education programs? A number of critics of gifted education have argued that bright children ought to be helping slower students, rather than maximizing their own achievements (Henry 1994).

The intersection between gifted education and special education students is unclear and often contradictory in recent civil cases, but court decisions have not improved the prospects for gifted education. Gifted students are not considered a protected group (Karnes and Marquardt 2000). The courts will require special education for a documented "disability," but special education for an identified "ability" is not required. And in at least one decision, *Wright* v. *Ector County Independent School District*, even simple grade acceleration, an inexpensive way to meet some needs of gifted students, may not be a legal option for a highly able learner. Nor do efforts to ensure fair minority representation in gifted programs appear to stand scrutiny by the judiciary (*Hampton* v. *Jefferson County Board of Education*).

The courts appear unwilling to enforce equality in educational opportunity for gifted students if that opportunity goes further than the egalitarianism enforced by public schools. One wonders, what happened to meritocracy?

Meritocracy, in which achievement is rewarded, is absent in modern U.S. schools. Two reasons stand out, one more insidious than the other. First, high-achieving students are exploited in the regular classroom for reasons that have little to do with the students' needs. They are used as tutors for those students who need an extra boost, as group leaders to enhance the quality of group products, as providers of high scores on state and federal standardized tests. Gifted students serve as statistical boosts for public schools that lack robust "Annual Yearly Progress" reports for "No Child Left Behind" mandates. And they anchor demographics, keeping students in their home districts, which is essential for state funding. Each element certainly works for the interest of the school district. Unfortunately, such practices do not benefit the individual gifted student.

The second reason involves the views that others have of gifted students. For example, school districts might not provide challenging classes for high-ability students because school administrators believe that these students will succeed regardless of the education they are provided. In this way, the district is absolved from the responsibility to educate these students to their ability. In fact, high-ability students, especially those from poverty settings, lose educational opportunity because their abilities are neither identified nor nurtured.

Gifted students need an education environment that requires hard work and persistence to reach high levels of problem-solving and experimentation. Without it, they lose motivation. When they are placed in an environment of education malaise and deprived of meaningful work, high-ability students cannot develop their cognitive and creative skill.

Gardner, Damon, and Csikszentmihalyi (2001) describe the experience of "flow," a point at which our skills and full mental capabilities match a challenge. When challenge is missing, students are placed in a downward spiral of dull activity. Students who are capable of high-level cognition learn to "tread water" until all class members are ready to go on. Some students wait, docile and compliant; others use negative behaviors to fill the time. All of these students learn to work on their own with no guidance or feedback from teachers. All end up wasting time on off-task activities. Bucking the routines of lock-step learning discourages these students and wastes the most precious resource of any democracy, intellectual capital.

All students of promise, identified by rigorous testing, must be offered advanced and accelerated learning options to maximize their potential growth. They must be fitted to become lifelong learners and problem-solvers par excellence, capable of great creativity and leadership. Only this path will increase American intellectual potential.

Equality is desirable, but not always defensible. Students who learn at a faster pace find themselves hamstrung when they must dawdle simply to keep in step with their classmates. True equal opportunity opens doors for all of the individual's potential. If schools allow individuals to run the curriculum at their own pace, to set high learning goals, to achieve rigorous standards, and to be guided by trained professionals, they will raise educational opportunity for all students. If three blind students and one sighted student come to class, equality dictates that all must be given identical resources. Do we take sight from the one to ensure equality of outcome, or do we provide equality of opportunity to enhance every individual's potential for fulfillment?

We can imagine Thomas Jefferson waiting at the University of Virginia, anticipating exemplary scholars selected from all corners and economic levels of local schoolhouses. He is waiting to meet those students who have risen above their classmates as a result of hard work and clear thinking. Instead, he receives a missive from schoolmasters who argue that it is unjust to identify one student as smarter than another. The schoolmasters declare, "No students will be advanced ahead of their classmates regardless of their ability. To do so would be most undemocratic." What would Jefferson say?

References

Ford, D., and Russo, C. "Meeting the Needs of the Gifted: A Legal Imperative." *Roeper Review* 17 (1995): 224-29.

Gardner, Howard; Damon, William; and Csikszentmihalyi, Mihaly. *Good Work: When Excellence and Ethics Meet.* New York: Basic Books, 2001.

Hampton v. Jefferson County Board of Education, 102 F. Supp. 2nd 358 (U.S. Dist. 2000).

Heller, K.; Monks, F.; and Paslow, A.H., eds. *International Handbook of Research and Development of Giftedness and Talent.* New York: Pergamon, 1993.

Henry, William. *In Defense of Elitism.* New York: Anchor, 1994.

Karnes, F., and Marquardt, R. *Gifted Children and Legal Issues.* Scottsdale, Ariz.: Gifted Psychology Press, 2000.

Marland, Sidney. *Education of the Gifted and Talented: Report to Congress.* Washington, D.C.: U.S. Government Printing Office, 1972.

Office of Educational Research and Improvement. *National Excellence: A Case for Developing America's Talent.* Washington, D.C.: U.S. Department of Education, 1993.

Renzulli, J. *The Enrichment Triad Model: A Guide for Developing Defensible Programs for the Gifted.* Mansfield Center, Conn.: Creative Learning Press, 1977.

Simon, John. "Introduction." In *Dumbing Down: Essays on the Strip-Mining of American Culture*, edited by Katharine Washburn and John Thornton. New York: W.W. Norton, 1996.

Wright v. Ector County Independent School District, 867. S.W. 2nd 863 (Tex. App. Ct. 1993).

SECTARIAN SCHOOLING AND CIVIC RESPONSIBILITY: "Social Capital" in Jewish Day Schools

CAROL HARRIS-SHAPIRO

When the public schools' role in promoting democratic engagement is discussed, sectarian schools often serve as a handy foil. Some blame what they see as students' selfishness, confusion, and apathy on the paucity of values education in public schools, noting in contrast the moral foundations of parochial education. Others congratulate the public schools for fostering tolerance of diversity, comparing this success to the divisiveness and bigotry religious school alumni allegedly bring to public discourse (Ravitch and Viteritti 2001).

We need to move beyond these caricatures if we are to discover the real potential of religious schools for developing good citizenship. Through analyzing the development of "social capital" with-

Carol Harris-Shapiro is an assistant professor of contemporary Jewish studies at Gratz College and coordinator of the graduate program in Jewish Communal Service. She was ordained at the Reconstructionist Rabbinical College and received her Ph.D. in religion from Temple University. She has taught in a number of schools, including Villanova University, LaSalle University, Philadelphia University, Rosemont College, and Temple University, as well as teaching courses for senior adults throughout the Philadelphia area. Recent publications include *Messianic Judaism: A Rabbi's Journey Through Religious Change in America* (Beacon Press, 1999). Harris-Shapiro currently is working on a study conducting in-depth interviews of American Jews and their understandings of God, faith, and spiritual matters.

in the Jewish day school movement, we may better understand the ability of such education to create active, empowered American citizens.

An ambivalent sentiment toward religious education is embedded in the history of the American public school. At one time all public education was intertwined with values and beliefs taken from the Protestant majority. Well into the twentieth century, public schools permitted Bible readings, prayer, and celebration of Christian holidays. Much like "White privilege," which is invisible to those who benefit from it, this "Protestant privilege" allowed public schools to inculcate Protestant values with the belief that this provided nonsectarian, American, moral instruction. Indeed, the common school movement was motivated specifically to Americanize immigrants and fight the factionalism of the Catholic influx. Only the teaching of common values, the argument went, could support our democratic institutions by inculcating a shared vision of the responsible American citizen (Baer 1987, p. 22). Thus, even while public education was imbued with religiously-based principles, its pedagogic purpose was to eliminate societal fragmentation and conflict stemming from religious separatism, from whence emerged both the present-day admiration of and the fear of full-time religious education.

Jews entering the United States initially gravitated toward sectarian schooling; but by the 1870s, full-time religious education was largely abandoned in favor of the public schools. However, in the 1870s and 1880s, in response to evangelical Christians insisting that the United States was a "Christian America," American Jews became more ideologically committed to the affirmation of a religiously neutral state government and education system (Sarna 1998, pp. 133-34). As Jonathan Sarna explains, "To attend public schools, and to guard them from sectarianism, became not just a matter of Jewish communal interest but, as Jews saw it, actually a patriotic obligation as well" (p. 134). As part of an ongoing attempt to maintain the high wall of church-state separation that would protect Jewish interests and allow Jews to take their place as equals in American society, Jewish organizations supported the elimination of the remaining Protestant teachings in the public schools (Dalin 2002, pp. 300-301). Instruction in Jewish religion, history, and culture was relegated to supplementary schools.

After World War II, Jews began to rethink this commitment to the public schools. Orthodox Jewish survivors of the Holocaust revived the Jewish day school as a viable option for Orthodox youth. And, more remarkably, in the 1960s and 1970s, non-Orthodox (liberal) Judaism began to sponsor Jewish day schools that combined Jewish and secular studies. Reasons for this development vary; parents were disappointed with the poor quality of Jewish supplementary schools, were frightened by substance abuse and violence in the public schools, and were worried about the increasing assimilation of Jewish youth into a non-Jewish world. Conservative and Reform day schools, which began during these decades, promised an intensely Jewish alternative in a liberal form that met the needs of these families (Wertheimer 1999, pp. 49-50). In 1956 fewer than one in 20 Jewish children attended religious day schools (Beinart 1999, p. 21). According to the recent *Census of Jewish Day Schools in the United States*, about 200,000 students are now in Jewish day schools, about one-third of all Jewish children. Approximately 40,000 of these are being educated in Reform, Conservative, or transdenominational Jewish community day schools (Schick 2000).

It now appears that the liberal Jewish commitment to universal public education as the cornerstone of American democracy has been shaken. Voices from non-Orthodox Judaism now raise the possibility of federal support of Jewish day schools through vouchers, tax credits, and other means (Wertheimer 2002). Does this trend indicate a retreat to safe communal boundaries? Is this the educational equivalent of a gated community, where people live comfortably behind high walls with only "their own kind"? Does creating rich Jewish education experiences through private school settings negate larger commitments to the nation and to fellow citizens?

In order to understand what is happening in Jewish day schools, a helpful place to begin is with Robert Putnam and his seminal research on "social capital" as the necessary ingredient to promote active citizen involvement. "Social capital," as Putnam describes it, comprises both the web of social relationships in formal and informal settings and "the norms of reciprocity and trustworthiness that arise from them" (2000, p. 19). Without these dense interpersonal relationships and the sense of confidence that one develops in one's fellow citizens, people are unwilling to come together to create social or political change. Putnam points out that the precipitous decline in associational behavior over the last 30 years, noted in almost all spheres of everyday life, has greatly affected American political health. We vote less frequently, are less involved in face-to-face political meetings and debates, and are more unwilling to shoulder the burden of public office (Putnam 2000, pp. 31-47). Other, related activities have fallen out of favor as well, including membership in civic organizations and religious organizations (pp. 48-79). Putnam argues that we need to nurture social capital to sustain American democracy, rather than leaving each individual to "bowl alone."

Jewish day schools certainly promote the formation of social capital. This is most marked among the families sending their children to non-Orthodox day schools. While Orthodox parents sending their children to Orthodox day schools have other sources for building interpersonal connections and trust (through tight-knit neighborhoods and Orthodox Jewish institutions required to fulfill their religious obligations), non-Orthodox parents, in contrast, may live in mainly non-Jewish neighborhoods, may or may not belong to synagogues or attend regularly, and may or may not send their child to a Jewish camp. In this case, it is often the Jewish day school that is a hub for formal and informal social ties.

Tracy Kaplowitz (2002) points out that day schools provide a common physical site, a sense of common identity for parents and children, and a sense of purpose to not only provide the best education to students but to strengthen Judaism in the process. When a student's adult relative becomes ill, often a formal committee from the school community will provide support with food and other aid. Family achievements often are celebrated in the school community. Formal social connections developed through parent-teacher organizations are complemented by informal friendship networks among children and their parents. Thus social capital is built through the interweaving of multiple social ties.

There is evidence that Jewish day school graduates continue active social networking within the Jewish community. For example, choosing a Jewish spouse has a strong effect on all other levels of Jewish communal involvement and thus is a key gateway to greater Jewish social capital (Mayer 1997). In *The National Jewish Population Survey, 2000-2001*, those with a day school education had an intermarriage rate of only 7%, compared to an intermarriage average of 43% for those who had no Jewish education and 23% for those who had a part-time Jewish education (United Jewish Communities 2003, p. 17). Steven M. Cohen (1999) demonstrates that day school education, independent of other factors, has a strong effect on intermarriage rates.

Other indicators support greater communal involvement from day school alumni. In a study of more than 3,000 day school alumni, ages 20 to 40, 82% attended Sabbath services regularly, and 65% were active or somewhat active in Jewish organizations (Schiff 1995). This compares quite favorably with the American Jewish population as a whole surveyed in the *NJPS 2000-01*, which shows only 28% of all Jewish adults ages 35 to 44 volunteer under Jewish auspices and only 32% attend a Jewish service at least monthly. It is even more unusual when one considers that the younger cohort studied by Schiff should have driven the numbers down, not up, because that is the age group less likely to join organizations and synagogues.

Although most of Schiff's respondents are alumni of Orthodox Jewish day schools who would be more likely to affiliate actively with the Jewish community, non-Orthodox alumni participate in the Jewish community in higher than average numbers as well. In a study of a transdenominational Jewish day school in Buffalo, New York, 69% of those graduating between 1964 and 1992 belonged to synagogues, 96% had connection to a Jewish community center, 90% contributed to Jewish charitable organizations, and 70% served on boards or committees of Jewish organizations (Dickson and Zakalik 2003).

This evidence demonstrates that Jewish day schools certainly promote what Putnam refers to as "bonding social capital," which consolidates social ties within a circumscribed community (2000, p. 22). Putnam postulates that religious congregations are especially good at creating social capital because attendees learn civic skills by running meetings and programs, they meet many others who will ask them to become involved in associations and causes, and it provides powerful social norms, theologically based, for involvement (pp. 66-67). Because day school education is associated with a much higher than average congregational affiliation rate for alumni, it would seem that such a link would encourage the extraordinarily high levels of involvement in the Jewish community noted above.

However, it is just this "bonding capital" that prevents some Jewish parents from sending their children to day schools. They express fear that the education the children will receive is too confined and parochial and that students will not learn to interact with non-Jews, a fear that may have some foundation. These reluctant parents, like other strong advocates of universal public school education, echo the philosophy of John Dewey in *Democracy and Education*: "The essential point is that isolation makes for rigidity and formal institutionalizing of life, for static and selfish ideals within the group" (1929, p. 99). In fact, much of the appeal of the Jewish day school is the "promise" that children graduating from this system will be more likely to marry a Jewish partner and raise Jewish children.

It is important to note that much of this debate depends on the definition of *diversity*. It is certainly true that religious diversity is more difficult to find in a Jewish day school than in a public school. But there are other, more fundamental types of diversity seen in the Jewish day school. For example, both wealthy and poor students are served by these schools. Unlike suburban public schools or private nonsectarian schools that draw primarily from the economic elite, Jewish day schools provide extensive scholarship programs to allow a significant number of students from underprivileged families to enroll. The Jewish day school body also is diverse in ethnic origin. Students who were born or whose parents were born in Israel, Russia, and other countries mingle with fourth- and fifth-generation Americans. The percentages are not insignificant; in Nahshon, a Reform Jewish day school, 20% of the student body is composed of Israeli and Russian Jewish children (Ingall 1998, p. 229). And as more and more Jewish parents adopt children of different races, racial heterogeneity also is beginning to appear in Jewish day schools.

In the day school, Jewishness is a common denominator that encourages friendships across class, national, and racial lines. This is unlike the "more diverse" settings of many public schools. Beverly Tatum (1997) describes the common phenomenon of students separating by ethnicity and race in public schools. She points out that, especially in adolescence, students from minority groups congregate separately as an act both of self-preservation and self-affirmation in the face of implicit or overt prejudice (pp. 59-71). Simply because a public school has a diverse population does not mean that students make friends across group boundaries, or even understand one another well. True diversity means more than population numbers.

My own experience illustrates this point. My public high school was approximately half-Jewish and half-Catholic, but it was not a setting that allowed the students to experience diversity in a positive way. Catholics and Jews attended different classes, sat in different sections in the cafeteria, and spent their leisure time in different parts of the school. Moreover, the animosity was so great that gang wars were fought between the two contingents; a year or so before I entered, a young man was stabbed in a lunchroom altercation. Far from learning from such diversity, I learned instead to fear and despise all Catholics, a response thankfully altered when I met my first roommate in college (and great friend) who is deeply Catholic.

In contrast to these dismal portraits of public school diversity, James Coleman and his colleagues (1982) show that Catholic schools, while having a lower ratio of African-American students to white students than do many public schools, integrate them more successfully in the classroom and support achievement for all students better than do private nonsectarian schools or public schools. One reason might be that the Catholic mission of the school provides a common basis to override certain forms of prejudice.

Attending a Jewish day school also does not automatically deprive its students and alumni of contact with non-Jewish cultures. Most Jewish day school alumni attend college, many complete graduate school, and a vast majority are fully integrated into the American work world (Dickson and Zakalik 2003, pp. 6-8). Moreover, while some students continue their Jewish schooling through high school and beyond, many, especially those raised in non-Orthodox settings, transition to public education at the beginning of middle school or high school. Jewish day school education is therefore not an "either-or." At some point in an individual's education, he or she will encounter and experience other cultures and other religions.

Many Jewish day schools make the balance between being "Jewish" and being an "American" a key component in their education philosophies. Schools seek not only to balance Judaic and general studies, but also to integrate these aspects of learning so that students can discover their identities as Jews *and* Americans. "Integration helps students understand how their distinctive Jewish voice can enliven the discourse in the American public arena, and how their understanding of American civic virtues can contribute to Jewish polity" (Zeldin 1998, p. 581). In the self-study of a Conservative Jewish day school in Atlanta, this balance is articulated: "We seek the harmony between our two powerful traditions, American democratic culture and Jewish teachings, by consciously integrating both into curriculum and school life. These values guide our ethical and educational decisions about the school and schooling, the learner and learning" (Epstein School 1991, p. 5).

This curricular imperative expresses itself in informal as well as formal learning opportunities. Day school students collect money for the American Heart Association, collect clothing to help the poor and refugees, gather Christmas toys for poor children, and give help to battered women's shelters. Some schools create exchange programs with inner-city school children or with other parochial schools (Shlossman 1996; Ingall 1998; Blustain 1997; Brown 1992). The Robert Saligman Middle School in Melrose Park, Pennsylvania, has had programs involving both its Jewish students and students from a Muslim school. More important, these students are taught that these projects helping non-Jews also fall under their responsibilities as Jews. "When a school collects clothing, books, canned goods, or money, it would be easy to let the good deeds stand for themselves. . . . But a Jewish day school has the opportunity to point out that as members of a community, we must provide for one another, even when we think our resources are limited. A secular school can say, 'Come, please participate,' while a Jewish school can say, 'Come, please participate because Judaism demands that we regard our community as extending beyond our immediate home and school'" (Levingston 2002, p. 55).

Despite these types of integration, it is unclear whether Jewish day schools create "bridging capital" among adult graduates. Bridging capital is the desire and ability to make social and organizational connections with those of different religious backgrounds. In studies of American Christians, being active in church does increase overall voluntarism, including volunteering for secular or community groups (Greeley 1997). However, full-time Christian schooling seems to have no effect on secular volunteering later in life, nor does belonging to a religious group as a child (Park and Smith 2000, pp. 281-83).

Information about American Jews points to just such mixed results. In a 1986 study of Jewish households in New Jersey, 35% of those who volunteered for Jewish organizations also volunteered for non-Jewish organizations (Rimor and Tobin 1990). However, results from the National Jewish Population Survey of 1990 (Kosmin et al. 1991, p. 35) found that fewer "Jews by religion" (those more Jewishly educated and more intensely involved in Jewish organizational life) than "Jews, no religion" volunteered for secular organizations in 1989, though the gap is small and perhaps not significant. This might indicate that the more one is involved in Jewish life, the less likely one is to volunteer in non-Jewish organizations; and Jewish day schools produce Jews more involved in Jewish life. On the other hand, this trend does not necessarily indicate a diminished interest in the outside world. In the *National Jewish Population Survey 2000-2001* (United Jewish Communities 2003, p. 13), more Jews who are highly affiliated with Jewish organizational life give charitable donations to non-Jewish causes (77%) than did unaffiliated Jews (54%). Other studies also have found that religious involvement has a positive effect on giving to non-religious organizations both among Jews (Rimor and Tobin 1990, p. 154) and among Christians (Nemeth and Luidens 2003). Although preliminary investigation of the *National Jewish Population Survey 2000-2001* (data provided by Jennifer Murphy of Temple University) shows a larger percentage of Jews with supplementary Jewish education volunteering and donating money to non-Jewish organizations than do Jewish day school alumni, the latter group still participates in healthy numbers. Approximately one-half of day school alumni volunteered in a non-Jewish organization over the past year, and more than one-third paid dues to a non-Jewish organization. It is perhaps a question of available hours and a belief that Jewish institutional needs are a priority, rather than disinterest or negative attitudes toward "the Other," that drives volunteer choices.

If Jewish day schools *do* prove to be better incubators of "bonding," rather than "bridging," social capital, would this endanger American democracy? Putnam and Feldstein (2003) argue that bridging social capital, connecting across diverse communities, is best accomplished when the diverse social elements see themselves, in fact, as "bonding." Bonding capital makes it easier to maintain strong, trusting, supportive ties; bridging capital develops when diverse individuals find a reason to bond. Bonding becomes the model of all good social capital. A person who knows how to bond within one's group has the skills and ability to forge new kinds of bonding across different class, ethnic, racial, and gender lines. However, one who avoids organizational associations would have a much more difficult time finding his or her place within any other organizational framework. Smidt explains, "Social capital serves to transform self-interested individuals exhibiting little social conscience and weak feelings of mutual obligation into members of a community expressing shared interests and a sense of the common good" (2003, p. 5).

Finally, what does this all mean for universal public education as the safeguard for democracy? Questions about social capital open the possibility that universal public education may not be the only path, or even the best path, to impart the disposition toward civic activism that is necessary for a thriving democratic culture.

This does not negate the vision of universal public education, which for most families will remain the norm either by choice or out of necessity. Nor does this call for specific remedies, such as vouchers to even the playing field between public and private education. However, full-time religious education should neither be feared as divisive nor idealized as saintly. Rather, we need to discover what kinds of private sectarian education help to produce good citizens willing and able to get involved in the public arena.

References

Baer, R.A. "American Public Education and the Myth of Value Neutrality." In *Democracy and the Renewal of Public Education*, edited by R.J. Neuhaus. Grand Rapids, Mich.: William B. Eerdmans, 1987.

Beinart, P. "The Rise of Jewish Schools." *Atlantic Monthly* 284, no. 4 (1999): 21-22.

Blustain, R. "Why More Parents Are Choosing Jewish Day Schools." *Moment* 22, no. 1 (1997): 58-62, 98.

Brown, S.M. "The Choice for Jewish Day Schools." *Educational Horizons* 71, no. 1 (1992): 45-52.

Cohen, S.M. "The Impact of Varieties of Jewish Education upon Jewish Identity: An Intergenerational Perspective." In *Jews in America: A*

Contemporary Reader, edited by R.R. Farber and C.I. Waxman. Hanover, N.H.: Brandeis University Press, 1999.

Coleman, J.S.; Hoffer, T.; and Kilgore, S. *High School Achievement: Public, Catholic and Private Schools Compared*. New York: Basic Books, 1982.

Dalin, D. "Jewish Critics of Strict Separationism." In *Jews and the American Public Square: Debating Religion and Republic*, edited by A. Mittleman, J.D. Sarna, and R. Licht. Lanham, Md.: Rowman and Littlefield, 2002.

Dewey, J. *Democracy and Education*. New York: Macmillan, 1929.

Dickson, S., and Zakalik, K.L. *Kadimah School: The Pursuit of Scholastic Excellence and Religious Commitment: Executive Summary*. Boston: Partnership for Excellence in Jewish Education, 2003. Available at: www.peje.org/KS-ExecutiveSummaryFINAL.pdf

Epstein School. *The Self-Study of the Epstein School, Solomon Schechter School of Atlanta, 1990-1991*. Atlanta, Ga., 1991.

Greeley, A. "The Tocqueville Files: The Other Civic America." *The American Prospect* 8, no. 32 (1997): 68-73.

Ingall, C.K. "The Nahshon School: Portrait of a Caring Community." *Religious Education* 93, no. 2 (1998): 227-40.

Kaplowitz, T. "Community Building: A New Role for the Jewish Day School." *Journal of Jewish Education* 68, no. 3 (2002): 29-48.

Kosmin, B., et al. *Highlights of the CJF National Jewish Population Survey*. New York: Council of Jewish Federations, 1991.

Levingston, J.K. "Day Schools on the Cusp: Women's League Outlook." In *Making the Case for Jewish Day Schools: A Compilation of Advocacy Writings, Volume II*, compiled by Shira Bolensky. Boston: Partership for Excellence in Jewish Education, 2002.

Mayer, E. "Jewishness Among the Intermarried." In *American Jewry: Portrait and Prognosis*, edited by D.M. Gordis and D.P. Gary. West Orange, N.J.: Behrman House, 1997.

Nemeth, R.J., and Luidens, D.A. "The Religious Basis of Charitable Giving in America: A Social Capital Perspective." In *Religion as Social Capital*, edited by C. Smidt. Waco, Texas: Baylor University Press, 2003.

Park, J.Z., and Smith, C. "To Whom Much Has Been Given: Religious Capital and Community Voluntarism Among Churchgoing Protestants." *Journal for the Scientific Study of Religion* 39, no. 3 (2000): 272-86.

Putnam, R.D. *Bowling Alone*. New York: Simon and Schuster, 2000.

Putnam, R.D., and Feldstein, L.M. *Better Together*. New York: Simon and Schuster, 2003.

Ravitch, D., and Viteritti, J.P. "Introduction." In *Making Good Citizens: Education and Civil Society*, edited by D. Ravitch and J.P. Viteritti. New Haven, Conn.: Yale University Press, 2001.

Rimor, M., and Tobin, G.A. "Jewish Giving Patterns to Jewish and Non-Jewish Philanthropies." In *Faith and Philanthropy in America*, edited by R. Wuthnow and V.A. Hodgkinson. San Francisco: Jossey-Bass, 1990.

Sarna, J. "The Jewish Experience in American Public and Private Education." In V*ouchers for School Choice: Challenge or Opportunity?* edited by M.J. Breger and D.M. Gordis. Boston: Wilstein Institute of Jewish Policy Studies, 1998.

Schick, M. *A Census of Jewish Day Schools in the United States*. New York: Avi Chai Foundation, 2000.

Schiff, A. "The Jewishness Quotient of Jewish Day School Graduates: Studying the Effect of Jewish Education on Adult Jewish Behavior." *Ten Da'at* 8, no. 1 (1995): 15-22.

Shlossman, R. "Can You Teach Empathy?" *Tikkun* 11, no. 2 (1996): 20-22.

Smidt, C. "Introduction." In *Religion as Social Capital*, edited by C. Smidt. Waco, Texas: Baylor University Press, 2003.

Tatum, B.D. *"Why Are All the Black Kids Sitting Together in the Cafeteria?" and Other Conversations About Race*. New York: Basic Books, 1997.

United Jewish Communities. *The National Jewish Population Survey, 2000-01: Strength, Challenge and Diversity in the American Jewish Population*. New York, 2003. http://www.ujc.org/content_display. html?ArticleID=94869

Wertheimer, J. "The Jewish Debate over State Aid to Religious Schools." In *Jews and the American Public Square: Debating Religion and Republic*, edited by A. Mittleman, J.D. Sarna, and R. Licht. Lanham, Md.: Rowman and Littlefield, 2002.

Wertheimer, J. "Who's Afraid of Jewish Day Schools?" *Commentary* 108, no. 5 (1999): 49-54.

Zeldin, M. "Integration and Interaction in the Jewish Day School." In *The Jewish Educational Leader's Handbook*, edited by R.E. Tornberg. Denver: A.R.E., 1998.

A MADHOUSE WITHOUT KEEPERS

Thomas S. Smith

My wife and I often go walking for our health in the small town of Marksville, Louisiana, where we have lived for almost 33 years. One weekend we were walking past the district attorney's office, and I noticed that an unfinished mural was on the side of the building. It included scenes of Louisiana and part of a quote by Thomas Jefferson. The next time we walked past the building, the mural was complete. All the words of Jefferson's quote were there: "If a nation expects to be ignorant and free, in a state of civilization, it expects what never was and never will be." This quotation is from Thomas Jefferson's *Letter to Colonel Charles Yancey*, 6 January 1816.

At about the same time, I saw the invitation to write an essay on the topic of public education, democracy, and the common good. The invitation asked whether the proposition of universal public education was still the mainstay of the common good and the only institution to ensure and sustain American democracy's

Thomas S. Smith has a B.A. from Northeast Louisiana University and an M.Ed. and M.A. from Louisiana State University. Currently he is pursuing a Ph.D. at the University of New Orleans. Smith was a teacher and administrator for the Avoyelles Parish Public School System for 33 years and was an adjunct instructor at Louisiana State University Alexandria and Northwestern State University of Louisiana.

good health, as education was thought to be in the early days of the American republic.

I have worked in the public school system for almost 33 years as a teacher and administrator and in post-secondary education as an adjunct college teacher of history for eight years. I am a true believer in universal public education as the surest support of the common good and the only institution that could ensure and sustain the good health of American democracy. Thomas Jefferson also said, "Preparation for the office of citizen is the crucial purpose of American education." I insist that this proposition is as valid today as it was in the early years of the American republic. I insist that this proposition must be believed and acted on by the American people today and in the future for American democracy to keep bearing the fruits of equality, common good, and general good health of the republic.

Horace Mann, a noted proponent of the common school movement, envisioned the common school as an equalizer. He agreed with other advocates of common schools that "educating all citizens is a fundamental necessity for a democratic society."[1] Mann believed that education was the basis of political stability and general social harmony. He held that public schools were fundamental to societal well-being, sound citizenship, and democratic participation. He observed, "A republican form of government, without intelligence in the people, must be, on a vast scale, what a mad-house, without superintendent or keepers, would be on a small one."[2]

The majority opinion in *Brown* v. *Board of Education* stated that education is a requirement for the performance of the most basic public responsibilities in American democracy. The opinion went on to say that education "is the very foundation of good citizenship" and that education is the prime "instrument in awakening the child to cultural values, in preparing him for later professional training, and in helping him to adjust normally to his environment."[3] An educated literate citizenry is what operates and safeguards American democracy. Without knowledgeable voters who can think critically, democracy loses it true essence and even its very being. The people must be literate enough to rule themselves and overrule forces attempting to produce inequality and injustice. Public education is the main instrument to making children aware of their cultural values and the cultural values of others in the American republic and elsewhere in the world.

In his 2001 Inaugural Address, President George W. Bush stated that Americans are "united across the generations by grand and enduring ideals. The grandest of these ideals is an unfolding American promise: That everyone belongs, that everyone deserves a chance, that no insignificant person was ever born." He said that ideals bind us together and that these ideals are what "move us beyond our backgrounds, lift us above our interests, and teach us what it means to be citizens. Every child must be taught these principles. Every citizen must uphold them."[4] Public schooling provides the key to these enduring ideals, and it is the responsibility of public education to enable every individual to make a contribution to the American republic.

There are some things important for democracy that only schools — not families, not religion, not communities, not society in general — can provide. For example, public schools make young Americans aware of their collective national identity by means of literature, holiday celebrations, and history lessons. In this country "schools bear a historic responsibility for the development of civic competence and civic conscientiousness within young citizens."[5] Fostering this collective national identity has long been an important facet of public schooling. The waves of immigrants were folded into the American population by the common schools.

Many Americans have assigned to America's schools the task of inculcating and nurturing the values — equality, social justice, civic responsibility, etc. — that Americans commonly hold sacred. The assumption is that equality and social justice and values of that sort must be taught carefully. Thus universal schooling has as a prime goal the enculturation of American students. John I. Goodlad says:

> it would be the height of folly for our schools not to have as
> their central mission educating the young in the democratic

ideals of humankind, the freedoms and responsibilities of a democratic society, and the civil and civic understandings and dispositions necessary to democratic citizenship.[6]

Goodlad exhorts us to teach students about democracy's political forms and structures, to inculcate democracy's ideals, and to provide opportunities to practice democratic ideals in daily life in school and in the real world. He emphasizes that the larger community must guarantee a democracy that will support and protect the democratic schooling that must take place within schools. If the larger community does not address certain democratic matters, those become the clear objectives of the public schools. Enculturation of American young as responsible citizens in American social and political democracy is a prime function of public schools. The larger community must ensure this function.[7]

In addition to values, schools build character. Amitai Etzioni says, "True character formation ought to be carried out largely in families and in the community; but even when these do their job to perfection, schools are needed to participate in what is a very demanding mission."[8] As a variety of data indicate, families and the community need assistance in forming children's character; and schools are necessary participants in this job.

Teaching democratic values and character is especially important in the United States as we try to join a very diverse citizenry into one nation. Undoubtedly, similar statements were made during the times of the great waves of immigration to the United States in the 1800s. Schools today must accept the same duty they performed in the 1800s, to teach understanding, tolerance, and good citizenry to young Americans in order for them to assume the responsibilities and challenges of a pluralistic republic. Those qualities do not come naturally. As Parker argues:

> Democratic living is not given in nature, like gold or water. It is a social construct, like a skyscraper, school playground, or new idea. Accordingly, there can be no democracy without its builders, caretakers, and change agents: democratic citizens. These citizens are constructs too. Who "builds" and cares for them?[9]

The answer is educators, but these educators must be empowered by the larger community. The community has an undeniably necessary role in sustaining the good health of democracy, and its role goes beyond just funding education. All citizens need to participate in schools and school issues, and they must be models of civic responsibility in the world outside the schools.

Perhaps the most important responsibility for our citizenry is to demand schools that are truly universal and public and then to support those schools with a passion. Our nation and its citizenry must not allow education to become elitist or inequitable. When education falls into the hands of the elite or of other special interest groups, it is no longer universal or genuinely public. Instead, it becomes a political act waged by some against others. When education is no longer public, then our nation may become, as Horace Mann warned, "mad-house, without superintendent or keepers."

This brings me back to the more personal side of this essay. As I said at the start of this essay, Jefferson's quotation on the mural inspired me. It was able to do so because public education enabled me to understand what Jefferson wrote. Universal public education — education for all, not just education for the elite — allowed me to rise out of the poverty in which I grew up.

As an educator for 33 years I have experienced much change and innovation in the field of education. I also have experienced the failings and seen the limitations of the general community, organized religion, and other interest groups in dealing with the development of all of America's youths. But over the years, I have seen the successes that universal public education produces: working men and women, loving parents, intelligent citizens. Universal public education works for the good of our republic and for the good of individuals. That is the simple beauty and the surest value of public education.

Notes

1. "Common School Movement," Abstract. http://www.academon.com/lib/paper/10297.html

2. Horace Mann, "Report No. 12 of the Massachusettes School Board" (1948). http://usinfo.state.gov/usa/infousa/facts/democrac/16.htm
3. Brown v. Board of Education, 347 U.S. 483 (1954).
4. "George W. Bush's 2001 Inaugural Address," 20 January 2001, pp. 1-2. http://usconservatives.about.com/bln0120inauguraladdresstext.htm?iam=momma_100_SKD
5. Kaye Pepper, "Strategies for Teaching Civic Education: An International Perspective," *Kappa Delta Pi Record* 40 (Winter 2004): 83.
6. John I. Goodlad, "Teaching What We Hold Sacred," *Educational Leadership* 61 (December 2003/January 2004): 20.
7. Ibid., p. 21.
8. Amitai Etzioni, "How Character Is Built," *Kappa Delta Pi Record* 40 (Winter 2004): 54.
9. W. Parker, *Teaching Democracy: Unity and Diversity in Public Life* (New York: Teachers College Press, 2003), p. xvii.

PUBLIC EDUCATION IS ALIVE AND WELL IN FAIRFAX COUNTY

DANIEL L. DUKE

Some Americans regard public education as a failed experiment, noble in intent but hopelessly flawed in practice. They acknowledge that public schools once were up to the challenges presented by a democratic society, but they go on to point out that today's schools are out of step in an increasingly competitive, information-age world. I will identify several assumptions held by critics of public education and test them against the track record of one public school system — Fairfax County Public Schools (FCPS) in Northern Virginia. Much of the information on which this essay is based was gathered in the process of completing a book on the organizational history of FCPS.

Fairfax, of course, is not just any school system. In 2004 it was the 12th largest school system in the United States, with more than 166,000 students and a budget that topped $1.5 *billion.* One of every seven public school students in Virginia attends an FCPS school. The school system, one of Virginia's largest enterprises,

Daniel L. Duke is a professor of educational leadership at the University of Virginia, founder of the Thomas Jefferson Center for Educational Design, past president of the University Council for Education Administration, and co-developer of the Darden-Curry Partners for Leaders in Education initiative. His latest book, *Education Empire: The Evolution of an Excellent Suburban School System,* will be published by the State University of New York Press.

employs more than 21,000 people to operate its 241 schools and centers, drive its 1,500 buses, prepare its 110,000 daily meals, and staff its sizeable central administration. The size of FCPS makes it an atypical American school system, but its rapidly changing demographics were cited by President Clinton as representative of the emerging American society. He suggested that Fairfax County would be an excellent place to study how people from increasingly diverse backgrounds live, work, and go to school together (Lipton and Benning 1997).

In my research on FCPS, I have come to believe that it is an excellent candidate for the nation's top school system. The reasons for this high praise will become clear in the paragraphs to follow. Fairfax successfully challenges many of the assumptions about public education held by critics. It is a school system that has met the challenges of growing diversity and not just held its own but raised performance. Ron Edmunds used to contend that the existence of only one inner-city school in which students achieved at or above grade level should compel people to reconsider their excuses about why students from poor homes are not meeting educational expectations. I feel similarly about Fairfax County Public Schools. The fact that at least one huge and highly diverse school system can succeed with all kinds of students — rich, poor, non-English-speaking, recently arrived, and so on — proves that diversity is not an insurmountable obstacle to high-quality public education.

Public Education Is Too Big and Bureaucratic

One central assumption of public education critics is that the enterprise has grown so large and bureaucratic that it can no longer respond effectively to the needs and interests of its clientele. For example, Ouchi (2003) has argued that big school systems often are characterized by dysfunctional organizations that resist meaningful change. Hill (1999) found that large school systems become bogged down in politics and lose their focus. Parents frequently fear that their children can easily get "lost" in a large school system and fail to receive the care and concern available in smaller, less impersonal settings.

Despite its size, Fairfax has managed to maintain the support of its patrons. Decades ago FCPS officials realized that the school system was growing so big that some measure of decentralization would be necessary. In the late 1960s four *area offices* were created, each with an area superintendent and a support staff. Area offices assumed responsibility for selecting school administrators, promoting school improvement efforts, handling special education matters, dealing with community concerns, and planning staff development activities. The area offices functioned reasonably well, but by the late 1990s Fairfax leaders felt that even greater decentralization was required. Instead of area offices, each constituting a large school system within a school system, eight *clusters* were created. Each cluster was made up of several *pyramids*, a pyramid consisting of a high school and its feeder schools. Cluster operations were streamlined, resulting in more decisions being made at the school level. For example, decisions about eligibility for special education services, which had been determined at the area office, were shifted to individual schools. Such moves meant that decisions directly affecting students were more likely to be responsive to parent concerns and local school needs.

Decentralization, of course, is hardly unique to FCPS. Most large school systems make some effort to decentralize typical central office operations. To ensure that decentralization makes a positive difference in the lives of students, Fairfax has gone a step further and created the Department of Educational Accountability (DEA). The DEA makes certain that every Fairfax school or center stays focused on the school system's goals. The goals are intended to ensure that every student receives a high-quality education. One goal, for example, states, "The percentage of students scoring above the national average on the Scholastic Aptitude Tests (SATs) will exceed last year's percentage, and the gap between SAT scores of minority and white students will narrow by 10 percent." Another goal states, "The percentage of students who take and pass Algebra I before the ninth grade will be increased, and the gap between white and minority students taking the course will be narrowed by at least 25 percent."

Prior to the DEA, various units in the central administration maintained databases related to student achievement and program effectiveness. By combining the offices of Educational Planning, Program Evaluation, Student Testing, and Minority Student Achievement under one umbrella, the DEA has been able to consolidate these databases and provide a single system for tracking the progress of individual students. Dubbed the Education Decision Support Library (EDSL), this massive database enables cluster directors, principals, and staff members to access information on individual students, groups of students based on particular characteristics, and students taught by a particular teacher. Thanks to the EDSL and its Instructional Management System (IMS), teachers can quickly determine how students are progressing with individual instructional objectives. Students who need assistance are identified and provided the help they require to keep from falling behind their classmates. The IMS even includes a test-item bank to enable teachers to construct sample tests and a collection of research-based "best practices" for use in designing instructional interventions. An additional component of the IMS is an Internet-based program for parents wanting up-to-the-minute information on their children's performance.

To make certain that the data available from the EDSL are put to good use, principals and teachers meet regularly to monitor how every student is doing academically. No longer is it acceptable to wait until report cards go home to discover that a student has experienced difficulties learning required material. When teachers in a particular school lack the skills to help struggling students, the Fairfax site-based management system enables principals to arrange for customized staff development. Principals also can call in a team of central office specialists assigned specifically to their cluster to assist in dealing with problems demanding intensive investigation and intervention.

Hoy and Sweetland (2001) have made the case that bureaucracy can be enabling as well as constraining. In the case of Fairfax, years of fine-tuning and re-organization have produced a central administration that is genuinely responsive to the needs of schools and students. Local taxpayers can take pride in the fact that the bulk of their contributions go directly to schools, not to maintaining a huge corps of bureaucrats. In 2003, 92.1% of all positions in FCPS were school-based and 88% of the annual budget went directly to schools.

Public Education Is a Monopoly Offering Clients Little Choice

Choice is considered an essential element of a free society. Critics characterize public education as a monopoly in which clients are compelled to take what they are given. In recent years, pressure has mounted to promote greater educational choice through vouchers and charter schools.

One of the benefits of Fairfax's enormous size has been its ability to offer students a variety of options at every level. The range of educational choices available to Fairfax students, in fact, could not be equaled in any nonpublic school or school system. FCPS constitutes a massive education market in which individual schools are encouraged to develop unique programs.

Among the options available to elementary students, for example, are focus schools, magnet schools, gifted centers, year-round schools, and foreign language immersion programs in French, German, Japanese, and Spanish. The two magnet elementary schools offer programs integrating arts, sciences, and technology. Students conduct research, produce live dramatic performances, compose original musical scores, design science experiments, and build museum exhibits. Partnerships with government agencies, museums, and universities enable the magnet schools to acquire expertise and resources normally unavailable to educators.

Even greater choice is found at the secondary level. Fairfax is the first large school system to offer an advanced course of studies to *all* students at every one of its high schools. Each comprehensive high school provides either an Advanced Placement or International Baccalaureate program. For students with exceptional talent, Thomas Jefferson High School for Science and Technology, arguably the top high school in the United States, is available. Students are selected for Thomas Jefferson based on their performance on an entrance examination. Students interested in entering the workforce after graduation can choose to attend one of Fairfax's five career academies. The academies focus on different career combinations, ranging from health and human services to engineering and scientific technology to communication arts. Participation in an academy program entails job shadowing and internships, as well as coursework.

Secondary students who have not experienced success in a regular school setting may attend one of several alternative schools designed to expedite credit acquisition. A full range of summer learning opportunities is available as well. Fairfax also operates the Online Campus, a Web-based course delivery system with courses identical to those offered in traditional classrooms. Arrangements with local colleges and community colleges make it possible for students to take advanced courses for credit toward high school graduation. The QUEST program is a three-year science, mathematics, language arts, and technology enrichment program for high-achieving minority students in grades six through eight.

Advocates of higher academic standards sometimes express the fear that increasing options may have a deleterious effect on student achievement. Fairfax has demonstrated that high standards can be maintained without standardizing every student's educational experience.

Public Education Cannot Accommodate Diversity

Some critics aver that public schools in the United States embrace and preserve white, middle-class culture. Students from other backgrounds are said to experience self-consciousness and a second-class education. They struggle to fit in and meet academic expectations.

It would be difficult to find a more diverse school system than Fairfax County Public Schools or one that has done a better job of addressing the needs of students from different cultural, linguistic, religious, and socioeconomic backgrounds. During the 1990s, Fairfax County welcomed almost 113,000 immigrants. The 2000 Census indicated that 237,677, or approximately one-quarter, of Fairfax residents were foreign born. While Hispanics accounted for 31% of this number, the largest percentage of immigrants — nearly half — came from Asia. A language other than English was spoken in nearly 30% of Fairfax homes. The major language groups included: Spanish, Korean, Urdu, Vietnamese, Arabic, Farsi/Persian, Chinese, Punjabi, Hindi, and Somali.

Beginning in the 1970s, Fairfax County Public Schools offered language-minority students a full program of English as a Second Language (ESL). At one point, the school system relied on ESL centers where language minority students were clustered until their English skills permitted them to attend regular classes. In recent years, however, the centers have given way to school-based ESL programs that allow non-English-speakers to be integrated with other students in nonacademic classes from their first days in school.

Even when the federal government mandated bilingual education in the 1970s, Fairfax resisted, arguing that its ESL programs had proven to be very effective. Eventually, under President Reagan, the Department of Education backed off requiring bilingual education. Fairfax's success with ESL programs was cited as a primary reason for this policy shift. As the number of immigrant children who are illiterate in their native language has increased, FCPS has recognized the need for more transitional classes to help these young people prepare for entry into regular academic classes. In addition, Fairfax operates a huge adult education program to assist the parents of these students in gaining proficiency in English.

Increasing diversity for Fairfax has meant greater numbers of poor students, as well as foreign-born students. Almost one of every four Fairfax students qualifies for free or reduced-price lunch. More than 2,000 county residents are listed as "homeless."

With poverty often come academic problems. Aware of the tendency of poor students to lag behind their peers, Fairfax adopted a policy of special needs funding in the 1980s. This policy allowed additional resources to flow to schools with high concentrations of poor and at-risk students. Two highly successful components of Fairfax's special needs initiatives have been Success by Eight and Project Excel.

Success by Eight calls for grouping students in kindergarten through second grade by skill level and interest, rather than age and grade level. By drawing on high-quality early childhood education practices and instituting full-day kindergartens, Success by Eight schools have largely achieved their primary goal of making every student a reader by age eight.

Project Excel initially targeted the 20 elementary schools with the largest percentages of students at risk of failing high-stakes state tests. Using supplementary resources, each school chose a "curriculum model" with a proven track record and made program adjustments aimed at ensuring that students were prepared for the state tests. Three years were permitted to implement new programs. Schools that achieved their benchmarks received bonuses for all staff members.

Programs such as Success by Eight and Project Excel have enabled Fairfax to do more than maintain performance levels in the face of increasing student diversity. What makes Fairfax so remarkable is that student achievement has continued to rise despite growing numbers of poor and minority students. Consider the following accomplishments listed on FCPS "fact sheets":

- More than 80% of all FCPS third-, fifth-, and eighth-graders passed the math Standard of Learning (SOL) tests in 2002.
- The passing rate for the SOL English exam for third-graders has risen from 68% (1998) to 82% (2002). Fifth-graders have increased their pass rate for the writing exam from 80% (1998) to 92% (2002).
- On the 2003 Scholastic Aptitude Test (SAT), FCPS students scored their highest ever (1110), 86 points above the national average.

The more than 23,000 special education students in Fairfax also have shared in the school system's successes. Ninety-two percent of students with disabilities graduate with academic diplomas. The remaining 8% receive special diplomas. Six out of 10 students with disabilities go on to post-secondary education following graduation. Fairfax truly is a school system for *all* students.

Public Education Cannot Achieve Both Equity and Excellence

To many critics, public education has sacrificed educational excellence in order to "level the playing field" and promote equal educational opportunity. Parents of bright students complain that their children are held back while teachers focus their energies on assisting less able classmates. If they can afford it, the most disgruntled of these parents opt out of public education in favor of private or parochial schools or home schooling.

Fairfax educators long have recognized that a truly *public* system of education must not exclude any segment of its public. As a result, there has been no large-scale exodus of bright students. Fairfax's advanced and honors offerings are as extensive as those of any school system. School-based programs for gifted students are available in grades K-12. In addition, full-time gifted centers have been created for exceptionally talented students in grades three through eight. At the high school level, Fairfax is the first large school system to offer a full honors program — either Advanced Placement or International Baccalaureate — at every one of its high schools. The jewel in the crown is Fairfax's internationally acclaimed magnet school — Thomas Jefferson High School for Science and Technology. Jefferson students are chosen on the basis of their performance on a rigorous admission examination. Staffed by exceptional teachers and supported by a variety of corporate sponsors, TJHSST can make a legitimate claim to be the top public high school in the United States.

As Fairfax's student body has grown more diverse, steps have been taken to expand access to challenging academic programs. For example, a new set of eligibility criteria was adopted to provide greater opportunities for at-risk students to participate in elementary gifted programs. Admissions policies for TJHSST are under constant review. To assist minority students seeking access to the prestigious high school, the Parent-Teacher-Student Association sponsors annual informational meetings and preparation courses for students desiring to take the admissions examination.

Perhaps the initiative for which Fairfax can be most proud is its new policy opening Advanced Placement and International Baccalaureate programs at every high school to any student who wishes to participate. To ensure that teachers in these rigorous programs provide assistance to all students, not just the brightest, Fairfax is the first large school system to require that every AP and IB student take the external examination associated with their course or program. Teachers are not permitted to encourage only their highest achievers to sit for the examinations.

There is ample evidence that Fairfax's focus on educational excellence is paying off. In 2003, 20,689 FCPS students took Advanced Placement exams, up from 20,236 in 2002. The number of scores of three or above increased to 13,278 from 13,089 the previous year. When *Newsweek* (Mathews 2003) identified the top high schools in the nation based on student participation in AP and IB programs, Fairfax was the only large school system to have every eligible high school in the top 4%. Six Fairfax schools ranked in the top 100. The implication is clear: Fairfax bends over backwards to challenge all students. Fairfax leaders are proving what education philosopher Thomas Green (1983) argued years ago — that public schools are more likely to achieve equity by pursuing excellence than they are to achieve excellence by pursuing equity. An exclusive focus on equity can lead, he maintained, to mediocrity, a result that fails to serve the interests of any student.

No clearer indication exists of Fairfax's commitment to challenging all of its students than Stuart High School. The Stuart student body reflects the demographic shifts occurring in Fairfax County. The school's enrollment of 1,450 students includes: Hispanics (30%), whites (27%), Asians (20%), Middle Easterners (12%), and African Americans (11%). Fifty-four percent of these students qualify for free or reduced-price lunch, and seven out of 10 were born outside the United States. The annual mobility rate (students moving into or out of school) hovers around 30%. Given the make-up of the student body, many people would not be surprised to learn that the performance of Stuart students on the first administration of Virginia's high-stakes, Standards of Learning tests in 1998 placed them last among Fairfax's 21 high schools. Five years later, however, Stuart students had risen to 13th, in the process passing several schools in very affluent sections of the county. Nine out of 10 Stuart students graduate from high school, and in 2002 a remarkable 99% of these graduates went on to enroll in two- or four-year colleges. In 2003, 40% of Stuart students enrolled in IB courses, and 80% of them achieved at least a 4 on the IB exam, exceeding the district average of 67%. Stuart students are performing two standard deviations above their predicted achievement, based on the school's poverty index.

Stuart's dramatic turnaround is testimony to what can be accomplished with a dedicated faculty, a supportive community, a visionary principal, and a school system totally committed to providing every student with a quality education. This combination of factors has enabled Stuart to take the steps necessary to raise student achievement. These steps included:

- Starting school early in August so students have an extra month to prepare for state tests in the spring.
- Convening groups of teachers on a regular basis to monitor student progress on curriculum goals.
- Initiating a phone service to contact persistent over-sleepers.
- Insisting that every teacher is a reading teacher.
- Operating special summer sessions for students who lag behind.
- Double-blocking Algebra I and Transitional English courses to provide struggling students with extended learning time.

The school system demonstrated its faith in Stuart's efforts by providing a computer for every 1.8 students and underwriting extensive program and staff development.

Reflections on a Great Public School System

The message of Fairfax County Public Schools is straightforward: Education for the common good depends on uncommonly good public education. The school system has not allowed its enormous size to prevent it from delivering high-quality programs to all students — from the most gifted to the disabled, from the recent foreign arrival to the capable student hoping to get into a good college, from the student requiring a nontraditional learning environment to the career-oriented young person seeking solid career preparation. As a consequence, Fairfax County Public Schools can lay claim to being the best school system in America — not the best school system in White America or the best school system in Middle-Class America; the best school system in America. Period.

Skeptics, of course, can argue that such pronouncements are easy to make for a wealthy county. While there is no denying the fact that Fairfax is one of the most affluent communities in the nation, it spends less per pupil than do a great many school systems — $9,961 in 2003-04. Nor can Fairfax count on the state for much assistance, because Virginia provides far less support for its public schools than do most states. Money does not account for Fairfax's impressive performance.

Fairfax, it must be admitted, has been the beneficiary of geography. Its location on the doorstep of the nation's capital has meant that it can draw from a very talented pool of teachers and administrators. Location also has meant high visibility, a sure lure for top-notch education leaders. Fairfax has been blessed with some extraordinary superintendents and central office personnel.

While absolutely necessary, an army of talented educators and capable leaders is not sufficient to explain Fairfax's success. Certainly there are dozens of other large school systems staffed by exceptional individuals. What ultimately sets Fairfax apart, I believe, are two critical factors: the community's high level of support for public education and the school system's unique organizational culture. The two are clearly related.

The citizens of Fairfax County, for the most part, still believe in public education. With few exceptions, they have supported their school system in good times and bad, approving huge bond issues so that the school system can provide the best facilities for its growing population and voting for county supervisors and, since 1995, school board members who are committed to maintaining an excellent school system. This voting record was most recently demonstrated in November 2003, when county residents soundly defeated a candidate for the Board of Supervisors who threatened to place a cap on property taxes. Despite the fact that Fairfax had been hard hit by the burst high-tech "bubble," people were not willing to place narrow self-interest ahead of their young people. Besides individual residents, Fairfax's corporate "citizens" also have actively supported public education with generous donations of money, personnel, and other resources. Corporate contributions have played a major role in the development of Fairfax's nationally acclaimed magnet schools and vocational-technical academies.

The second key to Fairfax's success is its organizational culture. Taking its cue from the community, Fairfax educators want nothing less than the best education that can be provided for the county's young people. This commitment manifests itself not in boastfulness and inflated claims, but in an openness to self-reflection, self-criticism, and innovation. Fairfax educators recognize that every program can be improved. No program is allowed to go unevaluated. The school system assesses every program on a continuing cycle and adjusts or eliminates ineffective initiatives. Teachers are engaged in action research, study groups, and professional learning communities in order to identify ways that instruction can be delivered more effectively.

Another important aspect of Fairfax's culture is an unwillingness to leave anything important to chance. Policies are carefully monitored to make certain they are achieving the desired effects. No one assumes that the public is aware of the good work being done in district classrooms. A regular effort is made to keep the community informed about the school system's accomplishments. Similarly, district officials do not assume that talented teachers and administrators will somehow find their way to Northern Virginia. Fairfax County actively recruits educators at home and abroad, provides them with top-quality staff development, and encourages those with leadership potential to enter one of the district's leader development programs.

A Concluding Comment

Like the nation in which it is located, the Fairfax County Public Schools were not born great. The school system's "story" is not a fairy tale. Fairfax got to where it is today because of hard work by a dedicated staff and strong support from the community. These sound like obvious ingredients for success, and perhaps they are. Yet if they are so obvious, why are there not more Fairfaxes? This is the question that policy makers, education leaders, and community leaders should be asking. Perhaps the No Child Left Behind Act (NCLB) will prompt such inquiry. What NCLB does that previous education improvement efforts did not do is place school systems squarely in the crosshairs. Past legislation focused on the teacher, the classroom, the program, and the school. NCLB recognizes that the likelihood of high-quality teaching, learning, and schooling depends on the quality of the entire school system. That Fairfax has been able to fulfill the promise of public education for hundreds of thousands of young people from diverse backgrounds serves as a beacon of hope for other school systems.

Notes

Green, Thomas F. "Excellence, Equity, and Equality." In *Handbook of Teaching and Policy*, edited by Lee S. Shulman and Gary Sykes. New York: Longman, 1983.

Hill, Paul T. *Supplying Effective Public Schools in Big Cities*. Washington, D.C.: Brookings Institution, 1999.

Hoy, Wayne K., and Sweetland, Scott R. "Designing Better Schools: The Meaning and Measure of Enabling School Structures." *Educational Administration Quarterly* 37 (August 2001): 296-321.

Lipton, Eric, and Benning, Victoria. "With Fairfax's Celebrated Ethnic Mix, Rewards and Problems." *Washington Post*, 2 October 1997, pp. D1, D5.

Mathews, Jay. "The Best High Schools in America." *Newsweek,* 2 June 2003.

Ouchi, William G. "Making Schools Work." *Education Week*, 3 September 2003, p. 56.